CLIMBING OLYMPUS

WHAT YOU CAN LEARN
FROM GREEK
MYTH AND WISDOM

STEPHEN BERTMAN, PH.D.

SOURCEBOOKS, INC.
NAPERVILLE, ILLINOIS

Published by Sourcebooks, Inc.
P.O. Box 4410, Naperville, Illinois 60567-4410
(630) 961-3900
FAX: (630) 961-2168
www.sourcebooks.com

Library of Congress Cataloging-in-Publication Data

Bertman, Stephen.
   Climbing Olympus : what you can learn from Greek myth and wisdom / by
Stephen Bertman.
      p. cm.
   Includes bibliographical references.
   ISBN 1-57071-929-2 (alk. paper)
   1. Mythology, Greek. 2. Philosophy, Ancient. I. Title.
BL785 .B475 2003
180—dc21
                                    2002153537

Printed and bound in the United States of America
VP   10   9   8   7   6   5   4   3   2   1

If one advances confidently in the direction
of his dreams, and endeavors to live the life
which he has imagined, he will meet a success
unexpected in common hours.

—Henry David Thoreau, *Walden*

Other Books by Stephen Bertman

Handbook to Life in Ancient Mesopotamia

Cultural Amnesia: America's Future and the Crisis of Memory

Hyperculture: The Human Cost of Speed

Doorways through Time: The Romance of Archaeology

The Conflict of Generations in Ancient Greece and Rome

Art and the Romans

Table of Contents

Acknowledgments

In traversing the gulf that separates past from present, I am indebted to two of my teachers, now deceased, Moses Hades and Gilbert Highet, who taught me that the shores of time are much closer than we might otherwise imagine, washed as they are by the waters of the human spirit. In inspiring me to sail those waters, I am also indebted to those many students across four decades who chartered my ship.

No literary vessel, however inspired, can weigh anchor today without a faithful first mate and able crew. My gratitude therefore goes to my literary agent, Ed Knappman, and to my editors, Hillel Black and Amy Baxter, for their commitment to this voyage. Special thanks also go to Diana Wu for plotting my course on her word processor.

PROLOGUE

ALIEN WISDOM

More than fifty years ago, on the evening of July 4, 1947, an incident is said to have occurred in the desert near Roswell, New Mexico. According to some who claimed to have seen the wreckage, an aircraft crashed that was not of this world. Fragments were found of an extraordinarily light-weight metal that, after being crushed by the hand, could spring back to its original shape. On one metal fragment an inscription was found written in a strange script unlike any other writing system on Earth. Survivors were found near the wreckage, but they were not human in form—survivors who would die soon after without telling their tale. What had crashed at Roswell was a space-craft from another galaxy, or even from another dimension, an extra-terrestrial vehicle that had taken an incredibly long voyage across both space and time. Or course, all of this is denied by official governmental sources.

But what if it all *did* happen? What if it was all true?

What might these aliens have taught us, these visitors from another world? What wisdom could they have conveyed about the universe, about life, perhaps even about ourselves?

Surely we would be fools not to listen, fools not to attempt a decipherment of the strange inscription, fools not to find and search the wreckage for more evidence of alien wisdom.

A Legacy That Waits

Such alien wisdom, however, is already available to us. Written in a strange script, it lies strewn through wreckage and has traveled thousands of years to reach our world. It is the alien wisdom of our own past that survives from a lost world that once existed on our own planet. It endures in the wreckage of buried cities and abandoned temples and in crumbling manuscripts that record a tongue last spoken more than twenty centuries ago. It is the wisdom of classical Greece.

Our mission, then, must be to recover the artifacts and literature of this lost civilization, to decipher the writing, interpret the words, and see if we can or should apply those antique teachings to our lives today.

But what is this supposed wisdom? And why is it "alien" to our world?

The Lessons of Greece

To begin, what are the teachings transmitted to us by the ancient Greeks? First, our lives are brief and fragile and, as such, too precious to waste. This lifetime is the only one we will ever have.

Second, we do not know who we are until we take time to discover who we can be. Hidden within us is unrealized potential. Hidden within us is a self we have yet to become. Next, we can only become that self with effort, with struggle. Each of us has a spiritual odyssey to undertake, a voyage across the sea of time.

We cannot undertake that voyage alone. We will need the help of others, the love of others, to reach port. And they will need *our* help and *our* love if they are to join us on the voyage.

There will be obstacles along the way and temptations—great obstacles and great temptations. There will be the temptation to give in to the current, to yield to the waves, to abandon our dreams. But the greatest obstacle, the greatest danger, will not lie outside us, but within: our willingness to remain who we are rather than become who we can yet be. Our greatest enemy is the enemy within, for hidden there are dark and destructive emotions. But also hidden there is the light of reason that can lead us to the dawn.

We must live with passion but beware of seduction. If forced to choose between a life of passionate commitment and a life of ease, we must elect passion over comfort. What matters most is not the gratification of our nerve endings but the nourishment of our soul. That is what separates us, and will always separate us, from the animals.

Worlds Apart

I have described this wisdom not simply as ancient, but alien. Why, then, is this so alien? Obviously, because it comes from a world that is not ours, a culture very different from our own. And since we have grown up in our culture, and live in it now, our conditioning prevents us from freely accepting these teachings as true. Instead, they seem foreign to our way of thinking, to the values our own culture has taught us.

We live in a materialistic society with more plenty than any society has ever known. Here the emphasis is on power and possession, on things, not on something as invisible as the human spirit. We are told that we are what we own, that happiness derives from the acquisition, ownership, and use of things, and that the more things we own the happier we will be. We are told this in words by commercial advertising, but we are also told this wordlessly by the images that surround us and the examples of success that are held high.

We live in a technological society driven by speed. Because of this we lack the opportunity to think and reflect on the meaning and purpose of our lives. Indeed, speed discourages us from thought and reflection by denying us perspective. Instead it gives us the exhilaration of sensory stimulation. It would be economically counterproductive, in fact, even subversive, if too many of us examined the unquestioned premises upon which our society is built. Instead, we are kept moving, our velocity sustained by corporate interests that profit from our addiction to speed.

Though our computers are crammed with data, they are devoid of wisdom. We have all the answers we'll ever need; it's the questions that we lack, the missing questions that, if found, could lend meaning and purpose to all the empty facts we possess.

Material and technological progress teach us that what is old is obsolete and useless. So we avert our eyes from the past and thus turn away from the very countercultural lessons that could serve as the means to our personal and social liberation.

The Death of Permanence

We live in a hyperculture, a culture moving too fast for its own human good. We are governed by the power of now, the power of an insistent present, uncompromising and uncompromised by any other dimension of time. It is the now of swift and unfeeling electrons.

In such a society, few things last or were ever meant to last. Instead, we are surrounded by flux. In such an environment, there are no grounds for passionate commitment, for there is nothing permanent to be committed to. Rare is a sense of obligation to one another, or a sense of obligation to anything that lies beyond the transitory self.

What we are witnessing in our time is the death of permanence, the death of those permanent things that were a source of comfort to people in ages past and a source of moral direction for humanity.

Even the past itself is being forgotten as our remembrance of history steadily declines. Afflicted by this cultural amnesia, the social equivalent of Alzheimer's disease, we are lost and confused among familiar surroundings.

Everywhere we go we are oppressed by urgency. But it is not a natural urgency to find our way again. Instead, it is an artificial urgency that impinges on our lives, an electronic urgency that requires us to respond at the speed of light to every external demand. And it is this same false urgency that is tearing at the fabric of our lives.

The Imperfect Greeks

The ancient Greeks did not have all the answers. They failed many times.

Neither they nor their world was perfect. The Greeks lacked most conveniences we know and many things we would regard today as necessities of life. And in those days life was more perilous and short than now.

Moreover, the Greeks often failed to live up to the very ideals they held high. Sometimes, in fact, they brought on tragedy in the blind pursuit of those ideals.

But the ancient Greeks asked questions—lots of them—and articulated those questions passionately in literature and art as has no other people. They took life seriously—not so seriously that they couldn't laugh at life or themselves, but seriously enough to turn the power of critical intelligence upon themselves and their shortcomings. Their legacy to us is those enduring questions.

A Challenge from the Past

The Greek philosophers ask us in our hurried pace to stop and think before we lose ourselves in all our rush, before we lose sight of the selves we could otherwise become. They ask us to transform our frenzied hyperculture into a humane culture before it is too late. But if we cannot save the world, they add, then let us begin by saving ourselves and those we love, for it is from such small and incremental changes that a new world can be born.

Lastly, the ancient Greeks remind us they are not aliens, but human like us. They remind us that if they, with all their imperfections, could begin a Golden Age, so can we. They ask us to board their spacecraft and continue their journey to the stars.

THE EIGHT PILLARS OF GREEK WISDOM

Each morning in Athens at dawn, the rising sun illuminates the entrance to the Parthenon, the most famous monument of ancient Greece. Erected atop the Acropolis, almost twenty-five centuries ago, the marble temple celebrates "the glory that was Greece."

Like the eight tall columns that still support the Parthenon's entranceway, there are eight ideological pillars that held up the edifice of Greek civilization, eight principles that explain its creative and enduring power.

Separately, each principle represents a single, dynamic idea. Together, the eight principles constitute an outlook that can transform our lives.

These are the eight pillars of Greek wisdom and their message to us:

Humanism:

"Be proud of your human abilities and believe in your capacity to achieve great things."

The Pursuit of Excellence:

"Try to be more today than you were yesterday, more tomorrow than you were today."

The Practice of Moderation:

"Beware of going to extremes, because in them lies danger."

Self-Knowledge:

"Identify and understand your weaknesses and strengths."

Rationalism:

"Search for the truth by using the power of your mind."

Restless Curiosity:

"Seek to know what things really are, not merely what they seem to be."

The Love of Freedom:

"Only if we are free can we find fulfillment."

Individualism:

"Take pride in who you are as a unique individual."

Through individualism we come to see ourselves as unique. Yet that uniqueness can only be realized through the love of freedom. In an environment of freedom we can employ a restless curiosity. By asking questions we strengthen our capacity for rationalism. By using reason we gain self-knowledge. With self-understanding we learn the importance of the practice of moderation and the pursuit of excellence. And in exercising both, we fulfill our potential, remaining true to the concept of humanism.

In each of the chapters that follow, we will explore each of these principles in detail and examine their implications for our lives. In our search for understanding, however, we will not be alone. The ghosts of the ancient Greeks will walk beside us, guiding us through the medium of their eternal myths and legends. Blazing the trail ahead will be gods and goddesses, heroines and heroes.

But before we can understand *what* the Greeks believed in we must first come to understand *whom* they believed in.

Gods and Humans: Similarities

The Bible tells us that God created man in His own image. The ancient Greeks, on the other hand, created the divine in their own human image, as their statues reveal. Nothing is clearer proof of their humanistic outlook. Indeed, it can be argued that if the Greeks believed in anything, it was themselves. Even the temples they built to honor the gods were visibly designed to celebrate man and his powers.

As their art shows us and as their myths tell us, the ancient Greeks endowed their gods with the physical and emotional attributes of human beings. Gods and goddesses looked like men and women, and like men and women they could love and hate.

Yet if the Greek gods had been mere replicas of humanity, they would not have been distinct from those who worshiped them. Besides the external and internal likenesses they bore to human beings, the Greek gods were marked by differences that set them strikingly apart from the human race. First, they were stronger; second, they lived forever.

It is not hard to understand how the ancient Greeks conceived of their gods in this way. Take the sea, for example, the natural element that embraces the Greek mainland and its islands. No matter how skilled or brave an ancient mariner might have been, he had to acknowledge the sea's immense power and he had to believe the sea had always existed, and would continue to exist, just as the land had. Thus the sea was all-powerful and eternal, the two distinguishing traits of the divine.

But to think of the sea as simply a powerful abstraction would not have allowed a Greek fisherman caught in a howling gale to pray for his salvation and trust that his prayers would be answered. Consequently, the

Greeks endowed the sea with human attributes—with ears to hear prayers and a will to acknowledge them. The Greeks thus humanized what would otherwise have been a heartless force of nature and, in so doing, made the cosmos more intelligible. Because people have names, the Greeks gave a name to the sea. They called it Poseidon, a god whom the Romans in a later day would name Neptune.

The gods the Greeks prayed to did not only represent elements in nature. The Greeks were as intimately familiar with war as they were with the sea. They were a people who battled, and their history is replete with devastating wars, the most famous of which was the war at Troy.

Like the sea, war is an eternal force with a superhuman will, an undying power with a life of its own. Recognizing this, the Greeks regarded war as divine. Yet for it to respond to the shouts of warriors or the cries of victims, war needed to hear and feel, and so was equipped by the Greek imagination with human senses. It was also given a name, Ares, by the Greeks, Mars by the later Romans.

In addition to natural elements like the sea or social agents like war, other forces—internal and therefore less visible—were granted divine status. One of these was the power of sexuality. Such a force, the Greeks concluded, had always been a factor in perpetuating life, sometimes in defiance of personal will and reason. The element of the erotic was thus eternal and omnipotent. But praying for sexual fulfillment required a force that could somehow hear their pleas and answer them. And so the Greeks conceived Aphrodite, the goddess of love, whom in later centuries the Romans called Venus.

Gods and Humans: Differences

Like so many other peoples of the ancient world, the Greeks did not think of the divine as a single entity, but as a group of separate powers each with its own realm and personality. At the same time, this attitude made the gods and goddesses of the Greeks different from the God of the Old Testament.

But Greek deities were different from the Biblical concept of God in another very important way. The Greek gods were in no sense morally superior to the human race. They did not demand, as did the God of the Bible, that human beings live up to a high standard of moral conduct, nor did they give man moral guidance—a set of Ten Commandments or a Sermon on the Mount. Were we to hold the Bible in one hand and a book of Greek mythology in the other, we would discover to our amazement that just about every one of the Biblical commandments were violated, not by the Greeks themselves, but by their gods. For example, there were gods who coveted, stole, lied, dishonored their parents, committed adultery, and murdered. In short, the Greek gods reflected human beings not only in their strengths, but also in their weaknesses.

A superficial reading of such an indictment might lead us to believe that the ancient Greeks were an immoral lot, inasmuch as their very gods were "sinners." But nothing could be farther from the truth. In actuality, the Greeks were passionately committed to understanding their moral place in the universe and developing a just and lawful society on Earth. In fact, their philosophers—the world's first—dedicated their lives to this ethical quest. The Greeks were guided in this pursuit by what they saw as a unique human attribute, the power of reason. And it was this pursuit, the humanly conceived and conducted search for truth, that ennobled them.

Building a Personal Temple

Each of us can be the architect of our existence. With the aid of the eight pillars of Greek wisdom, we can design a temple and a life we can be proud of.

[11]

Let us begin by reviewing the principles we encountered at the beginning of this chapter.

Individualism affirms the unique potential of our personality.

The love of freedom inspires us to actualize that potential.

Restless curiosity leads us to explore all its dimensions.

Rationalism gives us the means to solve problems and understand ourselves.

Self-knowledge informs us about our strengths and weaknesses.

The practice of moderation helps us balance our behavior.

The pursuit of excellence spurs us to achieve.

Humanism celebrates our efforts.

Working together like the pillars of a Greek temple, these principles can support the superstructure of our lives and guide us toward personal fulfillment. To be sure, like the pillars of a Greek temple, they must also stand upon a rock-solid foundation to do their job well. In human terms, this means we must also possess the basic knowledge and fundamental skills needed to put our philosophy into practice at home and in the workplace.

A Word before Construction

Before starting to build our own personal temple, let's pause to examine how the Greeks built theirs. To put it simply, they worked slowly and steadily, just as we should. Every part of a marble temple was made by hand, none of it by machine. The columns were carved with the same patience and skill as the sculpture.

The lesson here is not to be in a hurry, not to be hasty. It is the quality of the end product that is most important, not the speed at which it is made. The Parthenon, for example, took ten years to complete, and its sculptures another six, yet it has endured for almost twenty-five centuries.

Each column, moreover, was made of separate drums, one stacked on top of the other. Constructing a marble pillar then, like constructing a pillar of belief, is an incremental process: we begin at the bottom and ascend to the top in measured steps, making certain that each successive component is carefully and deliberately fitted to the one below.

Naturally, there must be a master plan to which the parts conform. But life is not perfect, and the execution of every plan may involve delay. Therefore, commitment is essential, especially for a project that is long. But as stone rises on stone, flagging spirits will rise too as the ideal takes visible form.

No temple was ever built by a single individual; they were built by a team. Accordingly, in building our personal temple we will need to borrow the love, strength, and understanding from at least one other human being. If we are blessed, our efforts will be shared. And if life does not permit us to finish the work, the work may yet go on in the hands of others who have learned our dream.

Deconstruction and Triumph

Some Greek temples stand incomplete for reasons we cannot fathom. Others have been ravaged by time, the hostile forces of nature, or the willful intent of men. In the early Middle Ages, the Parthenon was converted into a church and, later, into a mosque. In 1687 it was serving as a Turkish ammunition dump when a lucky cannon shot from a Venetian frigate scored a direct hit, detonated the gunpowder inside, and blew both architecture and sculpture to smithereens. (A giant hole from the explosion can still be seen in the Parthenon's south wall.) In the decades that followed, the occupying Turks pillaged the marble, using statues for target practice or selling them to the passing traveler. One such traveler, Lord Elgin, bought sculpture by the yard and shipped it to London, where—to the annoyance of modern Greeks—it was kept in the British Museum. Today, a contemporary assault by acid rain eats away at the Parthenon's walls. Throughout all these vicissitudes the temple has endured as an indomitable symbol of an ancient spirit. Its triumphs over such odds can serve to inspire us as we attempt to erect a structure of our own.

CHAPTER 1

THE FIRST PILLAR

HUMANISM

The Challenges of Humanness

Unlike the codes of the ancient Near East that stressed the need for humility and obedience and the smallness of man in the face of divine authority, Greek practice held that the proper posture for humanity was not prostrate but upright and tall.

Indeed, the Greeks viewed man as potentially superior to the gods. The gods had everything, yes. They were omnipotent and exempt from death. But by his very weakness, man was a greater thing. Since only human beings could risk and lose, only human beings could appreciate the meaning of achievement. Since it was man who must die, it was only man who could most truly live. While the gods were static and unchanging, humanity possessed the capacity for growth, and in the experiencing of that growth, human beings could take the truest measure of existence.

The gods dwelt in their palace atop Mt. Olympus, continually taunting man with the precious qualities he did not possess, immortality and absolute power. Had the gods' home been invisible, had they lived in a heavenly kingdom beyond the power of human sight, that would be one thing. But they did not. By being within man's reach, but not within his full grasp, by being so like him in so many ways, the gods by their very existence tempted humanity to become more godlike.

The Choice of Achilles

No one in myth felt this torture more cruelly than Achilles. His father, Peleus, was a mortal; but his mother, Thetis, was a goddess. Thus Achilles was born of two worlds, but belonged fully to neither. Stronger than other men, he was still mortal like all other humans. And so he craved what he was denied—everlasting life—even if it had to be purchased at the price of life itself.

When he was a young man, it is said, he was given a rare privilege by the Fates, who controlled all destinies. They let him choose the length and outcome of his life. He could live to a ripe old age in his father's palace and then die peacefully in his sleep, but he would never be remembered. Or he could be remembered forever, but for this he would have to die while young. The long life would contain little worth remembering; the short life would burn into the memories of all who came later.

Achilles chose the short life of undying fame. Only in that way could he achieve the immortality he had been denied by birth.

Even when he was born, his mother feared the harm that might befall him, and so she carried him to the sacred river Styx in order that she might bathe him in its divine waters. Baptism in the Styx, you see, would make his skin invulnerable to any wound. But as Thetis dipped the infant into the waters of the river, she held him by his heel. It was that part of his body that the waters of the Styx never touched, and thus his heel was not protected by the river's magic power.

Later, when Achilles grew to manhood, he fought in the Trojan War, despite the wishes of his mother who still feared for his safety. Her fears were realized when, near the end of the war, Achilles was struck by an arrow in his heel, the one vulnerable part of his body. Though the wound itself seemed minor, it was from that wound that young Achilles died as the Fates had decreed.

Though each of us is far weaker than the mighty Achilles, each of us is like him in one respect. All of us have a weakness we cannot see, a weakness that can be our undoing. Yet were we without such weaknesses, we would cease to be human. To be human is to be vulnerable. Only the gods cannot be wounded, but the gods cannot love or feel as intensely as we can.

The Temptation of Ulysses

Achilles was willing to pay the price of death in order to live on in the memory of others. Another warrior who fought beside him at Troy, Ulysses, was willing to pay a similar price, but for a different reason.

On the way home from the Trojan War, Ulysses was shipwrecked on the island of the goddess Calypso. There she fell in love with him and he with her. Her island, tropical and lush, was the most remote in all the sea, and for the two, Ulysses and Calypso, it was a paradise all its own, and they its only inhabitants.

Calypso knew that Ulysses, a mortal, must someday die, and would have to leave her to make the journey to the land of the dead. Therefore, the beautiful goddess offered him eternal life through the gift of nectar and ambrosia, foods of the gods. Accepting her offer would free Ulysses from the prospect of dying, and he would live forever, enjoying the pleasures of the senses forevermore by her side.

But for weeks after her offer, she found him weeping by the seashore, looking out toward the horizon beyond which lay the home he had not seen for twenty years.

It was not his home itself that made him weep, or yearning for his wife, or for his infant son now grown to manhood during the long years Ulysses had been away at war and at sea. It was the knowledge that they needed him, needed his presence, needed him to right the wrongs that had befallen his home and kingdom in the years of his absence. Only by returning could he become husband, father, and king once again, by acting as only he could act, filling the empty space he had left behind.

Ulysses rejected Calypso's offer to become a god and thus escape death. To escape death in this way would mean to relinquish life. There on Calypso's island where everything would be predictable and secure, available and free, one thing would be missing: a future into which Ulysses could hurl himself with all of his being.

Our lives exist, the Greeks believed, in order that we may complete an unfinished task, and it is by that task—even dimly glimpsed—that our lives are given meaning whatever the peril.

Calypso offered Ulysses everything he was, but denied him everything he might become. There on that blessed isle, blessed but desolate, a god might live—but not a man. With good reason, the goddess was called Calypso, a name that means "she who hides," for had Ulysses stayed with her and lived with her evermore, he would have been hidden, hidden from others, yes, but also hidden from himself, from the self he could be.

In the end it was not home Ulysses sought, carried on the waves by his raft, but what he could become. Watching him as he dipped in the troughs and rose in the swell, slowly paddling seaward, even Calypso understood.

In Praise of Life

Humanism is the proud affirmation of both our promise and our duty. Because of the pride they felt in being human, the Greeks celebrated the human enterprise with all of their talent and might in pictures and stories. With a kind of poetic justice, those celebratory acts gave their race the immortality nature denied it. Greek literature and art live on, battered by time but indomitable and still defiant. Among all these works the common denominator is our species' tale—the struggle against great odds for self-realization.

Animating the Inanimate

This affirmation of life is clearly evident in the pottery of the ancient Greeks. Though a vessel of baked clay could hold as much liquid whether it was beautiful or not, the Greeks expended great time and energy in endowing their pottery with symmetrical form and harmonious decoration. This is all the more remarkable since, unlike statues and temples of marble, pottery is so fragile. But the Greek response to this observation would have been that life itself is a fragile thing. Should we not then commit ourselves wholeheartedly to shaping our lives? they would ask. Should we not then fill our lives with harmony? To demonstrate this conviction, they painted the surfaces of their vases with images of life, at first the deeds and lives of heroes, and then vignettes from their very own everyday lives: working, playing, loving. In so doing, they gave life to what had been lifeless, transmuting what had been inanimate clay into an animated declaration of life's infinite possibilities. In the miniature universe of the painted vase, the sun of humanity blazed.

Just as with pottery, so with coins. Like pottery, coins could serve a practical function without being lovely to look at: it would have been enough if they had simply been lumps of metal the purity and weight of which were guaranteed by the state through the use of an official mark. But the Greeks took what had been a crude Near Eastern invention and recognized its aesthetic and symbolic potential. What better "mark," they thought, than the human face that could be so harmoniously framed by the coin's circular rim. At first, each Greek city chose the face of its patron god or goddess and later, after Alexander the Great, the faces of its kings, to decorate its coins. But, either way, when the Greeks held coins in their hands it was their own human image they saw reflected back at them.

What the Greeks did was make the world over in their own image, an image visible as well in the statues and monumental sculptures that populated their cities, and the man-made environment of their minds. "Man is the measure of all things," proclaimed the philosopher Protagoras.

An Ode to Humanity

In the fifth century B.C., an Athenian playwright named Sophocles praised humanity's achievements. He wrote:

> Many are the world's wonders, but none more wondrous than man.
> Under the south wind's gale, he traverses the gray sea,
> knifing through its surging swells.
> Earth, eldest of the gods, imperishable and everlasting,
> he erodes year after year with winding furrows
> cut by his equine team.
> The winged flocks of birds,
> the wild herds of beasts,
> and the salt-sea schools of fish
> he entraps in the woven mesh of his devious net.
> With his devices he overpowers the creatures of the wild,
> reining in the shaggy-maned stallion
> and yoking the stubborn mountain bull.
> Speech he developed and wind-swift thought
> and the talent to dwell together, and learned
> how to evade the chilling frost and pelting rain.
> Ingenious, there is nothing that comes he cannot master.
> Only from Death can he not contrive an escape.

The Test of Humanism

In the almost twenty-five centuries since those words were written, the human race has extended its triumphs beyond the mere mastery of sea or land, bird or beast. Through technology we have become godlike in our powers. We are still subject to death, but advances in medicine have prolonged our lifetimes even as advances in science may someday slow or even halt the process of aging. Nor is it only longevity that has been amplified. The quality of human life, not just its quantity, has been enhanced in myriad ways. As a result, the average person today knows pleasures and comforts once reserved solely for the ancient gods. Calypso's island is no longer just a dream.

But like Ulysses, we now must make a decision. We must decide whether the avoidance of pain and the seeking of pleasure is all that life asks of us. We must decide whether our only obligation is to ourselves, or whether—beyond the island's beach—there is a farther shore, one that we need as much as it needs us. That world may not need more gods, but more humanness. It asks us not to hide the selves we can become.

In meeting this challenge, we face many obstacles the Greeks never knew, not whirlpools or three-headed monsters, but newer forces that conspire to rob us of our humanity by asking us to be less than we are—a technology that increasingly replaces the warmth of human contact with the cold efficiency of machines; a marketplace that persuades us that we are only as important as the things we own; and a government that by its bigness convinces us that we are too small to effect change.

Yet all of these things—technology, marketplace, and government—are human creations. Anything humanly conceived, the Greeks are quick to remind us, can be humanly changed if there is enough personal commitment and collective will. Our task then is nothing less than to reclaim our humanity, both as individuals and as a society. And if we are to change society, we must start with ourselves.

Practicing Humanism

Putting humanism into practice in our everyday lives requires that we define the term accurately.

To many today, the term "humanist" is synonymous with the word "atheist"; a humanist, in effect, is someone who doesn't believe in God. But that is not what the term meant in its classical sense. The ancient Greeks most emphatically believed in man, but they also most emphatically believed in the divine. If not, they wouldn't have built temples or had myths. What made their belief special was that they looked into human nature and saw its godlike potential. Socrates, for example, may have been tried and executed for not worshipping the traditional gods of Greece in traditional ways, but there was no man more fervently and conscientiously committed to the spiritual mandate carved over Apollo's door: "Know thyself."

Following in Socrates's footsteps, we should pursue his favorite hobby, the serious business of definition, a little farther. Underlying the word "humanism" is the distinction between two other words: "human" and "humane." As biological beings we are, *de facto*, human; but to be humane requires effort. Implicit in "humane" is the notion that there are latent sensibilities in our character that must be cultivated if we are to attain our fullest stature. That task, the Greeks would have argued, is the moral imperative of our existence.

Ironically, the words "human" and "humane" are not even Greek; they come from Latin. It was the Romans who were humanized by their contact with Greek culture, and they went on to transmit Hellenic ideals to the world they ruled, translating them along the way into their own tongue. The Greeks themselves might have used a different word, *paideia*, by which they meant the civilizing process of education. In the universities of medieval Italy, a new Latin word, *humanitas*, came into fashion, referring to those studies (language and literature) that could liberate the mind. Today, we would call them the liberal arts or humanities, and it is through them still, beginning with the languages and literatures of ancient Greece and Rome, that we can best discover our human and humane potential.

Humanism thus implies a commitment to the special abilities and talents we possess as human beings. To practice humanism in a personal way means first to look into ourselves to discover the particular abilities and talents that are ours. The second step is to actively apply them to our everyday lives. Yet just the recognition of our potential can set us on the right path.

Initially, we should take stock of our lives and draw up a personal inventory. What are the things we have done in the past that make us proudest, the things that have given us the greatest satisfaction? What are the qualities that others respect us for, the things in us they admire and love? Too often the trivia of daily life, or the rush of events, prevents us from being the kind of people we have it within ourselves to be.

In taking this self-assessment, we may come to see that our fulfillment as individuals depends, at least in part, on our engagement with the outside world. Becoming fully humane thus means opening ourselves to the needs of other human beings. Becoming a "humanitarian" really doesn't require great riches; it only demands a great heart.

It is not Easy Street, moreover, that we should be looking to live on, but a street that asks more of us than we are accustomed to giving, because only then can we grow.

The ancient Greeks were quick to admit there are forces that prevent our self-realization, forces that try to stop us from being the kind of human beings we can become. But all that means is we must struggle all the harder. This is what the German poet Goethe, long an admirer of the classics, meant when he said near the end of *Faust*, "Freedom and life are only earned by those who conquer them each day anew." Until we recognize our own intrinsic worth as human beings we will not make such an effort.

The ancient Greeks did not labor under the illusion that after all that effort there would be a heavenly reward. Neither should we if we are to remain true to their faith. Accepting that this is the only life there is can have one of two effects. It can induce a sense of gloom about life's limits, or it can challenge us to transcend those limits in the knowledge that this is the only chance we will ever have to get it right.

Humanism is a philosophy of limitless possibilities tempered by the fact that we must someday die. It is marked, as H.D.F. Kitto once wrote, "by the tension between these two forces, passionate delight in life, and clear apprehension of its unalterable framework."

Rather than advising us to concede defeat, humanism urges us to strive for victory.

Humanism, however, doesn't mean merely accepting ourselves for what we are. It doesn't automatically impress the stamp of self-esteem upon our lives. Instead, it obligates us to develop the potentialities we have uncovered. Humanism, then, is not a gift, but a responsibility.

Chapter 2

The Second Pillar
The Pursuit of Excellence

The second pillar of Greek wisdom is the pursuit of excellence. In the grammar of the Greek universe, humanity was not a noun, but a verb: moving, changing, evolving toward a fuller realization of its inner potential. This is something no god could ever experience or know sitting smugly atop Olympus.

Humanism, the first pillar of Greek wisdom, was not pure self-congratulation, applauding humanity for what it was, but implied a dynamic and progressive process of spiritual growth. This process was the pursuit of excellence.

The Heroic Code
In the final year of the Trojan War, a warrior named Glaucus stopped and stood on the bloody battlefield to explain what motivated him to fight. He declared:

> Hippolochus bore me, and from him I claim my birth.
> He sent me to Troy, and told me straight and true:
> "Always excel and outdo the others,
> and don't make your ancestors ashamed."

In these verses the epic poet Homer captures the driving spirit of Greek civilization: the pursuit of excellence, the compulsion to be the best. For the warrior who spoke these lines, this pursuit was a necessary component of a hero's code, the unwritten law by which all warriors lived and died as had their fathers and grandfathers before them—to be the bravest, to be the best, whatever the cost.

But for the ancient Greeks, the pursuit of excellence grew to extend beyond the military battlefield to other, less warlike fields of endeavor. Indeed, had the Greeks been willing to settle for mediocrity in those other things, they would not be remembered today.

From Olympus to Olympia

Mt. Olympus, the tallest mountain in Greece and the home of the Greek gods, is located in northern Greece. But in southern Greece lies another place with a similar name, Olympia, the home of the Olympic Games.

Greek tradition records that the Olympic Games began in 776 B.C., about five centuries after the fall of Troy. According to legend, the Games were founded by none other than Hercules, the most famous muscle man in Greek mythology.

Though his mother, Alcmene, was a mortal, Hercules's father was Zeus, the king of the gods. Thus, like Achilles, Hercules's parentage was mixed—part human, part divine. This helps to explain his superhuman deeds, but it also explains why his story endeared him to the ancient Greeks. The part of him that was human made him kindred to humanity and inspired the Greeks to believe that they too could perform deeds that transcended the normal limits of human nature.

In fact, that is what the Olympic Games were really all about: showing the gods what human beings were capable of doing if they bent mind and muscle to the task. The Games were meant to honor Zeus, not by human sacrifice, but by human achievement. They were energized by the principle that man could best serve the gods by developing his own innate talents, in the process expanding the definition of what it means to be human. In effect, the proudest offering of the Greeks to their gods was themselves in all their mortal glory. More than merely sports, the Olympics were a ritual of supreme religious importance. Yet, as we have seen before, the true religion of ancient Greece was humanism, the worship of humanlike gods by men who strove to be like gods.

Held for more than a millennium until abolished in the fourth century A.D. by a Christian emperor of Rome, the ancient Olympics were a living testament to the pursuit of excellence. Though the land of Greece was often torn by war, every four years a sacred truce was declared so all communities could send representatives to compete. The prize for winning an event was a simple wreath of wild olive leaves. Though the prize had no monetary value, it earned the victor and his community the highest prestige, an immortality conferred by individual achievement and preserved forever in communal memory.

The original event of the first Olympics was a simple footrace. The length of the race was a *stade*, the Greek term for a distance measuring about two hundred meters. From that term came the word "stadium," the name for the place where the race was run. The stadium at Olympia was a plain, rectangular dirt track, shouldered by grassy slopes where spectators sat. A long channel inlaid in marble marked the line where the runners toed up, while a stepped pedestal was reserved for the judges.

Because the stopwatch hadn't been invented, races were not timed. The only thing that mattered was who crossed the finish line first. In fact, there were no "silver" or "bronze" medals; runners-up earned no glory.

Eventually, a variety of running competitions was added to the basic race—longer races, a relay race with torches, and a race in which contestants wore armor. Over the centuries, other events were added as well—the long jump, boxing, wrestling, javelin throwing, and chariot racing, plus two combination events called the pentathlon and the pancration. But the simple footrace always remained the premier event.

Besides being a religious occasion, the Olympics served the practical needs of military preparedness. Almost every event applied the skills needed in war, just as training for the Olympics provided an incentive for honing skills that could someday be used on the battlefield.

The most famous examples of Greek running, in fact, occurred in wartime. When the mighty Persian Empire prepared to invade Greece in 490 B.C., an Athenian runner by the name of Pheidippides ran from Athens to Sparta to appeal to the Spartans for aid. In doing so, he covered the 150 miles between the two cities in just two days. Then he had to run back to Athens with the Spartans' answer. As it turned out, they were eager to come, but out of religious scruples couldn't set out until the full moon.

With the help of their neighbors, the Plataeans, the Athenians then marched to the point on the coast where they thought the Persians would land, a place called Marathon. Charging at a run with spears in hand, they caught the Persians by surprise and drove them into the sea. A runner, perhaps Pheidippides himself, then ran nonstop cross-country from Marathon to Athens bearing news of the sensational and crucial victory. According to tradition, after reaching Athens and delivering his report, the runner collapsed and died. From the approximately twenty-six-mile length of that historic run, the "marathon" race of modern times was born.

Of all the Olympic events, however, there was one that had no military payoff—the throwing of the discus. Yet while discus throwing had no practical application, it equaled other events in its symbolic significance as proof of the pursuit of excellence. Indeed, the very impracticality of the event underlined its symbolic value all the more.

This value was given visual expression by a fifth century B.C. sculptor named Myron, who created a statue depicting a discus thrower perfectly poised between windup and release. In the statue the coiled pose of the athlete incarnates in its arms and bent back both the curvature of the round discus and the upcoming trajectory of its flight. In creating his masterpiece, Myron sought to portray not a particular discus thrower, but the ideal discus thrower, a consummate embodiment of physical excellence and its pursuit. But such excellence was not automatic; for its attainment self-discipline and determination were required. Only with training and concentration could the athlete reach his goal. Through these means, his potential would be liberated and actualized for all to see. Though militarily irrelevant, the throwing of the discus belonged in the Olympics because it demonstrated in a purer form than any other contest the passion of the Greek soul for perfection.

The most sacred place at the sanctuary of Olympia was Zeus's stone temple. Filling up the interior was one of the Seven Wonders of the Ancient World, the gold and ivory statue of the divine king seated upon his throne. Carvings in marble illustrating examples of physical prowess from Greece's mythic past adorned the temple's exterior.

Among the decorations were twelve sculpted panels celebrating the Labors of Hercules, Zeus's son and founder of the Olympic Games. According to legend, to expiate his sins Hercules was enslaved to a king and was required to do the king's bidding. The king in question conceived a series of daunting missions for Hercules to undertake. The eleventh took him to the edge of the earth where mighty Atlas stood and supported the heavens with his shoulders. Hercules had to obtain the Apples of the Hesperides, which could only be picked from the tree by

Atlas. But to free Atlas for this task, Hercules had to substitute for him and hold up the sky. The twelfth and last Labor took Hercules to the kingdom of the dead to fetch the fierce watchdog that guarded its gates. Hercules did so, according to one account, by feeding the beast dog-food laced with a sleeping potion. Though the Labors of Hercules were larger than life, his struggles to achieve the seemingly impossible and his determination not to quit in the face of challenge after challenge made him—along with his all-too-human imperfections of character—a role model for mortals striving to do and be their best.

Olympia, however, was not the only place in Greece where competitions were held to honor the gods. At Delphi, northwest of Athens, the god Apollo was so honored. The rocky ruins of his temple still stand beneath the towering heights of Mt. Parnassus, as do the remains of a stadium. Buried by an avalanche of stone from the mountainside, Delphi was excavated by archaeologists in the nineteenth century. Among their discoveries were works of sculpture including a life-sized bronze statue of a victorious charioteer still holding in his hands the reins of his winning team.

Such victors were honored not only by works of art that commemorated their victories, but also by poems that sang their praise. The Greek poet Pindar has left us just such a poem exalting a charioteer who won his race at Delphi. Among its verses are these:

> Humble when humility requires, proud when pride allows,
> I shall serve the destiny that preoccupies my mind,
> honoring it with all my might.

These lines, better than any others, express the inner justification for the Greek pursuit of excellence: the belief that within the human soul is a divine spark, and it is the duty of each of us to fan that spark into a flame.

Wine and Inspiration

Athletic competitions were not the only kinds of contests the Greeks held to honor their gods. They engaged in intellectual competitions as well.

To show their gratitude to Dionysus, the god who gave humanity the gift of wine, the people of Athens held a festival in his honor every spring. The central feature of the festival was a series of dramatic performances.

Drama was an invention inspired by the fertile imaginations of the Greeks. In the earliest days, a circular earthen floor used for the threshing of wheat became the world's first stage. At first, performances consisted of choral singing, but then a storyteller named Thespis (from whose name the word "thespian" comes) gave a speaking role to one of the chorus' members, thereby creating drama's first actor. Eventually a second actor was added (by the playwright Aeschylus) and finally a third (by Sophocles).

Though written especially for the festival, the plays did not just deal with Dionysus. Instead, they covered the full gamut of human experience, examining personal strivings and weaknesses, emotional conflicts between individuals, and the never-easy relationships between gods and mortals. Sometimes human experience was viewed from a comic perspective, but more often from a tragic one.

To offer the very best to Dionysus, the festival was designed competitively with prizes awarded to the best playwrights, the best actors, and the best producers—a communal acknowledgement of the pursuit of excellence and the historic precedent for today's Academy Awards. So powerful was the incentive and so gifted were the Athenians that the dramas they created not only inspired the plays, films, and television shows we enjoy today, but they continue to be performed in their own right as perpetually relevant and incisive statements about the human condition. It is a testament to the intellectual level of the ancient Athenians that these plays were attended not only by an elite coterie of theater-goers, but also by a city-wide public that packed the seats of Dionysus's theater at festival time.

It was Dionysus who became the patron god of theater, in part because of the country wine festivals that inspired the first choral songs, but also in part because the gift of wine freed people of their inhibitions and enabled them to forget their sorrows and think larger thoughts.

Like the drinking of too much wine, the pursuit of excellence does not guarantee a happy outcome. At the competitive festival of Dionysus, just as at the Olympics, there were always more losers than winners. Competitive striving always implied the risk of loss, but the ancient Greeks were congenital risk takers. It is no accident that the leading characters of their tragedies were heroes, for heroism often courts tragedy. This is because the hero's life is a life lived at the outer edge of experience. At such an extremity, success becomes an intoxicant that can cause the individual to lose perspective on his own human limitations and in the end pay a higher price than he would ever have imagined. But to dare less would be to know less and to be less, an alternative the Greek culture rejected.

One of the most beautiful vases to survive from antiquity is a Greek wine cup dating to the sixth century B.C. On its inner surface we see Dionysus triumphant over pirates who tried to kidnap him in the mistaken belief he was mortal. The god reclines in their abandoned ship, larger than life, floating tranquilly on an invisible sea. On the outer surface of the wine cup stand the painted figures of warriors on a battlefield, fighting to retrieve the corpse of a fallen comrade from the hands of enemies who seek to despoil his body of armor.

Inside, the wine cup exalts the image of a god who is all powerful and exempt from death; outside, it sings a hymn to man whose life and powers are finite and fragile, but whose days are precious precisely because they are so few. To be human is to suffer, but thereby know a sweetness no god can measure.

It is said that when the god Dionysus was a baby he was devoured by huge monsters called the Titans. Later, when the Titans tried to wrest Zeus's throne from him, Zeus fought them and blasted them with his fiery thunderbolt, reducing them to ashes. Out of these ashes, the story goes, Zeus fashioned man.

Thus, it is said, within man is a particle of the divine substance of Dionysus that the Titans had consumed. Like the kernel in a grain of wheat, this divine particle is contained within a brutal Titanic husk. Our task, then, is to liberate the divine energy in us imprisoned within its envelope of Titanic darkness.

The pursuit of excellence can be this process of liberation, as we struggle upward from the earth that pulls us down and strive toward the heights of Olympus.

The Meaning of Excellence

To be sure, we cannot all be winners, but neither were the Greeks. We may not throw the discus the farthest or write a prize-winning play. But that is not what life asks of us. Instead, it asks us to discover those things we are capable of doing well, and then to do them with all our heart and soul. The ancient Greeks never mistook winning for heroism. Like Hector in *The Iliad*, a person could be a hero even though he lost the war.

To be a hero, to pursue excellence, is to be a loving mother, to be a compassionate husband, to do our job well—whatever it may be—with honor, integrity, and passion. To do so is to fulfill our finest nature; to do less is to lose our chance to experience the full meaning of being alive.

The Price of Excellence

To pursue excellence, however, almost inevitably means to encounter frustration, and frustration, for the ancient Greeks, was the cruelest punishment of all.

Their notion of hell was strikingly different from our own. In the Greek version of hell, few people were tortured. In fact, only three were: Tityus, Sisyphus, and Tantalus, each guilty of a major crime against the gods. Tityus was tied spread-eagle to the ground as a vulture perpetually ate at his liver. Sisyphus was required to roll a boulder up a hill, but just as he reached the crest the boulder would always slip from his grip, tumbling to the bottom of the hill from which it again had to be rolled up. Tantalus was eternally hungry and thirsty, and was compelled to stand in a pool of cool, clear water beside which hung the bough of a tree laden with luscious fruit. Each time he bent down to get a drink of water, the level of the pool would drop; each time he reached out for a piece of fruit, a breeze would blow the bough away.

The three punishments, each unique in its own way, were united by a common theme, the theme of frustration. Tityus, struggle as he might, was unable to swat the vulture away; Sisyphus was unable to push the rock over the crest; and Tantalus was unable to eat or drink, the very food and water he sought being within his reach but beyond his grasp—the origin, incidentally, of the word "tantalize."

For the ancient Greeks, frustration, not physical pain, ranked as the ultimate punishment because they were a race of achievers. Just being in the land of the dead constituted punishment because nothing could ever be accomplished there. In its dark and dank environment, the dead dwelt as disembodied ghosts, devoid of substance and purpose.

Nor was Hades meant only for sinners; instead, everyone was consigned there. As a result, without a heaven to hope for, the ancient Greeks lived life with passionate intensity, knowing it was the only existence they could ever hope to enjoy. If the price of excellence was frustration in the here and now, it was a price worth paying. Without the savor of success the rest would be empty indeed.

No wonder the lives of Greek heroes so often ended in tragedy: they were frontiersmen, testing the perilous limits of human possibility. And that is also why they were so admired by their countrymen.

Not only did the pursuit of excellence lead to frustration, it also led to an often self-destructive competitiveness that plagued Greek civilization throughout its entire history, inciting factionalism, jealousy, and war. Yet without the pursuit of excellence and its fruits, the civilization of the Greeks would not be worth remembering.

It is the choice of Achilles, but it is our choice too, individually and collectively, to wallow in the warm mud of mediocrity, or climb to the mountain's cold and rocky heights. Indeed, when a hero fell from those heights and died, he was honored by his fellow warriors through funeral rites that featured competitive events in which prizes were awarded to the winners. The Greeks believed the best way of honoring a dead hero was to emulate the life he had led.

The Cost of Success

Those heights could be perilous, not just during the ascent but even at the summit. Achievement instills pride, but pride—as the Bible shrewdly observes—"goeth...before a fall."

Niobe and Arachne

Niobe had six daughters and six sons and boasted of the fact, comparing herself to the goddess Leto, who only had one daughter and one son. Leto's divine children, Apollo and Artemis, then took their revenge, shooting all of Niobe's children to death with arrows before their mother's eyes. Niobe learned her lesson. But like so many other tragic figures in Greek myth, she learned the lesson too late.

If our car hurtles off a cliff, it may be instructive to reflect then on the need to take slick hairpin turns more slowly, but it does us little good—a peculiarly mordant form of driver education that can at best benefit others by our tragic example. So it was for Niobe.

Arachne was another errant driver. Arachne boasted she could weave better than Athena, and even challenged the goddess to a competition. As it turned out, Arachne's weaving was flawless, as even Athena had to grudgingly admit. But the insult was too much for Athena to bear. She turned Arachne into an ugly spider, who would continue her weaving forever as a miniaturized and repulsive image of her former self. Even today we call spiders "arachnids."

The twin myths of Niobe and Arachne teach us the perils of getting too big for our britches. Once we let our accomplishments go to our heads, once we lose our humility, the universe pays us back. Metaphorically translated in Greek, "Every cloud has a silver lining" becomes, "Every silver lining has a cloud." In short, wrapped around every success is the risk of presumptuousness. That dark perception is at the core of the Greeks' vision of tragedy: the very impulse that drives us to succeed can push us over the edge. The assumption that we are exempt from consequences makes those very consequences more likely and real.

The Arrogance of Agamemnon

During the planning process for the attack on Troy, Agamemnon was appointed the Greek army's commander-in-chief. As the Greek fleet waited for their orders, King Agamemnon waited for a favorable wind to carry his ships across the sea. But the wind did not come. Meanwhile, the troops were getting restless and supplies were running low.

Agamemnon decided to turn to the army chaplain, a seer named Calchas, for advice. "It's your fault," Calchas said. "Once when you were hunting, you bragged you could throw a spear better than Artemis. She heard that, and now is taking her revenge. If you want to sail to Troy, you'll need to appease her."

"How do I do that?" Agamemnon asked.

"By sacrificing the life of your daughter," the priest sternly replied.

Agamemnon now faced a tough decision. If he did not sacrifice his daughter, Iphigenia, the fleet would never sail, and he would be humiliated in the eyes of his subjects. And, not incidentally, Agamemnon and his subjects would never get their hands on Troy's gold. Yet, for the mission to succeed, he would have to sacrifice his daughter's life. In the end, Agamemnon chose the love of glory and gold over the life of his child, and laid her upon the sacrificial altar.

Agamemnon's wife, Clytaemnestra, never forgot her husband's brutal decision. During the war, she conspired at home with a paramour to murder Agamemnon on his return. She even had beacon lights set up all the way from Troy and posted a sentry on the roof of her palace at Mycenae to watch for the signal of Troy's fall so she could set the wheels of the conspiracy in motion at the earliest possible moment.

When the war was over and Agamemnon came home, he had the effrontery to bring his mistress home with him. Clytaemnestra rolled out a royal purple carpet for him to walk on as he proudly stepped down from his chariot, and cunningly invited him to take a warm and soothing bath.

Once he was in the tub, Clytaemnestra and her lover, Aegisthus, threw a net over Agamemnon and hacked his body to pieces with their swords. Thus Agamemnon paid in blood for his self-centeredness and heartlessness.

Though Niobe, Arachne, and Agamemnon paid an extreme price, their stories taught the Greeks the dangers of excessive pride. The lesson for us is the same. Whatever our achievements, we mustn't let them go to our heads, or we too may pay a severe penalty.

Pursuing Excellence

Before pursuing excellence, a personal inventory is in order. What are we good at? What do we do well? In reaching for excellence, it is these things we must concentrate on and perfect.

And if the list is short, there's no need to worry. All it may mean is we haven't looked hard enough. What we are talking about is personal strengths, not necessarily heroic in size, and personal weaknesses that we can turn into strengths.

What races, so to speak, have we run where we've stopped short of the finish line, not because we were out of breath, but because we were out of caring? The pursuit of excellence means doing our very best at whatever we do. If there is no external reward, it doesn't mean we shouldn't do the job well. Personal satisfaction is, in the long run, far more important than getting the approval of others who live outside our skin.

Nor is the pursuit of excellence the same as achieving. The operative term is "pursuit," the act of trying. It was Woody Allen who once said, "Ninety percent of being a success is just showing up." How many people truly "show up"? How many students in a class show up physically, or mentally? How many employees show up determined to put in an honest day's work? How many people "show up" for life, whatever their role may be? That too is the meaning of excellence, to be the very best we can be in whatever role we have chosen or whatever role life has assigned us.

Many people do just enough to get by. If enough people behave that way, it's only natural for us to conclude that that's the way *we* should act too. But if so, we will be selling ourselves short, imitating people who will eventually die without discovering who they are.

Excellence to the Greeks was physical and intellectual, developing their bodies and developing their minds. Being intellectually lazy is as easy as being physically lazy: just as we can let the muscles of our body atrophy by not using them, so we can let the muscles of our mind grow weak. All the more reason to devote as much attention to exercising our minds as our bodies.

Education should not end with a graduation ceremony, for it is a lifelong pursuit. We must carry on—by independent reading, reflection, and discussion—what Robert Maynard Hutchins once called "the great conversation," a dialogue "that began in the dawn of history and that continues in the present day." The time spent in a gym must be matched by time spent in a library. If we do excel at something, we must also be mindful of the Greek maxim not to be too proud. What we have done will always fall short of what we might have accomplished.

CHAPTER 3

THE THIRD PILLAR
THE PRACTICE OF MODERATION

The third pillar of Greek wisdom is the practice of moderation.

The pursuit of excellence may become so absorbing that we lose sight of the rest of our lives in a compulsive rush to reach our goals. The ancient Greeks recognized this fact and counseled that we seek balance and avoid extremes.

So important was the need for moderation that it was inscribed above the entrance to one of Greece's most revered sanctuaries, the temple of the god Apollo at Delphi. The inscription, carved in stone, read *Mêden ágan,* "Nothing in excess."

The Risks of Flying

The island of Crete was once ruled by a tyrannical king named Minos. Serving him was his royal architect and engineer, an inventive genius named Daedalus, a man not unlike Leonardo da Vinci in a later age.

Minos believed Daedalus had betrayed him. (The story of the betrayal will be told in chapter 5.) Minos had Daedalus arrested, along with Daedalus's young son, Icarus.

Minos meditated upon the right punishment, most certainly ending in death, though the means had not yet been devised. For the time being, the king imprisoned Daedalus and Icarus in Daedalus's observatory atop the palace; there was only one exit and it could easily be guarded.

Fearing death, not so much for himself (for he could almost readily accept it), but more so for his son, Daedalus searched for a way to escape. Then one day he saw birds flying past his window and conceived a bold plan. Taking chunks of modeling wax from his workbench, feathers from his pillows, and slender branches from the young trees that grew on the balcony, Daedalus fashioned two sets of light wings. These he tied to his son's arms and then to his own. Daedalus patiently showed Icarus how to flap his arms like a bird. For days the two exercised and practiced until the testing time had come.

"My son," Daedalus cautioned, "you must not fly too low, or else the salt spray of the sea will wet your wings and weigh down the feathers, making them too heavy to lift. Nor must you fly too high, or else the heat of the sun's rays will melt the wax and the wings will come apart."

Then, at the father's signal, the two, standing at the roof's edge, dove into the empty air. The guard standing far below did not even notice their twin shadows sweeping across the marble pavement at his feet. He did not even turn to look into the blazing sun to see what birds could cast such great shadows.

Higher and higher the two soared, like eagles skimming over the island's surf-washed coast, heading toward open sea and freedom. Farmers gazed up from their plows, shepherds from their flocks, sighting the wonder above them as men for the first time flew.

Thrilled by liberation and the power of flight, young Icarus soon forgot his father's words of warning and flew higher and higher. Toward the sun he climbed until the wax of his wings grew soft in the sun's heat and the wings began to melt. Icarus struggled for a time, beating his arms faster and faster, until he plunged twisting and spinning into the waves below, and the sea's swell swallowed his body and rolled on as it had before.

No longer hearing his son's voice behind him, the old inventor turned to look back, to see where his son might be, scanning the sky as he rhythmically beat his own wings, searching the sky in anxiety, while far below tiny waves hid Icarus forever.

Over the years the ancient scholars of Greece drew lessons from this tale. Some observed that human beings often dare to do great things, but do not fully recognize the perils of their enterprise. Others wisely noted that the middle course is best. Fly too high and we encounter the sun's fatal heat, too low, the deadening spray of the sea. Thus, they advised, in our lives we must seek the Golden Mean, the safe middle between otherwise dangerous extremes. Moderation in all things is best.

A Perilous Passage

The test that extremes pose is illustrated by the adventures of Ulysses. To get back home from Troy, his ship had to sail through a strait set between two cliffs. In a cave in one cliff dwelled a six-headed carnivorous monster; at the foot of the other cliff swirled a huge whirlpool, deep and black. The monster could snatch up Ulysses's crew from the deck of his ship, while the whirlpool could swallow the ship whole. As he maneuvered through the strait, Ulysses had to decide which cliff to sail closer to. He chose the side of Scylla, the monster, rather than Charybdis, the whirlpool, reasoning that it was better to lose some of his crew than the entire ship and all its men. Sometimes in navigating the perilous passage between Scylla and Charybdis, we must choose the lesser danger and pray we make it through.

A Wall Too Far

Extremes can exist not only in sky and sea but also on land. Achilles, the most feared warrior of Greece, had a friend named Patroclus. Unlike the self-centered Achilles, Patroclus was compassionate. At one point in the Trojan War, Achilles stopped fighting for the Greek cause and held back the troops under his command. The reason: he had been insulted by his commander-in-chief, Agamemnon, a man he loathed for his arrogance. But Achilles's withdrawal from battle had dire consequences for the rest of the Greek army.

As the casualties mounted and their camp was under attack, Patroclus came to Achilles to ask a desperate favor. "If you won't fight," he pleaded, "at least let *me* go out. And let me wear your armor. When the Trojans see it, they'll think you've returned to battle and will pull back, at least for today."

Still nursing his grudge, Achilles reluctantly agreed, but on one condition. "Whatever you do, don't press as far as the city walls. Save that for me, if I ever go back. Don't steal my glory."

This said, Patroclus strapped on Achilles's armor and went out into combat. A brave warrior in his own right, he fought valiantly, aided by the illusion the armor created, an illusion that put fear into the hearts of the enemy. But just as Icarus, intoxicated by flight, flew higher and higher, so Patroclus, exhilarated by the prospect of total victory, drove farther and farther toward the fortress walls of Troy.

Then a god struck him down: Apollo, who warns us of the dangers of excess. Apollo struck him mightily on the back, stunning him and knocking the helmet from his head. After that, the Trojans finished Patroclus off with spear and sword.

What caused his death? In part delusion, for he became as much the victim of Achilles's armor as the men he slew, imagining that he was greater than he was. But he was also victimized by the very pursuit of excellence that can drive a man too far.

Had he only held the middle ground, he would have been safer. But it is hard to see the middle when you are blinded by emotion, and harder still when the middle is an invisible line, not as clearly defined as Icarus's sun or sea. All Patroclus could see was the wall, the wall that marked the destination, and the fatal end, of his dream.

Of Love and Its Denial

Of all the Golden Means we might seek, the hardest to find are those that lie within. In searching for the mean between psychological extremes there is no handy yardstick, no facile calculator we can employ. Hippolytus learned that lesson to his sorrow, as Euripides tells us in a play.

The Tragedy of Hippolytus

As the son of King Theseus of Athens, Prince Hippolytus worshiped Artemis, the virgin goddess of hunting. At the same time, he scorned her opposite, Aphrodite, the goddess of erotic love. Worshipping virginity, he rejected intercourse and marriage. For this, Aphrodite vowed to punish him. To accomplish her will, she made Hippolytus's stepmother, Queen Phaedra, fall madly in love with him.

Guilty over her sexual obsession, Phaedra confided in her maid, who advised her to act on her feelings. But on the grounds of conscience and loyalty to her husband, Phaedra rejected this advice. The maid, however, disclosed Phaedra's secret to Hippolytus in the hope that he would be sympathetic and gratify Phaedra's desire. Instead, he was shocked by what he heard. When Phaedra discovered what the maid had done, her shame drove her to commit suicide, but not before she left a note behind for her husband Theseus, laying the entire blame for what had happened on Hippolytus. After finding his wife's body and reading the note, Theseus cursed his son, who died cruelly at the hands of heaven.

[45]

As the playwright makes clear, Hippolytus's sin was not his worship of the virgin Artemis, but the exclusivity of that worship. The play teaches that neither divinity should be renounced; both should be acknowledged and respected for the power they represent. Indeed, had Hippolytus instead worshiped Aphrodite to the exclusion of Artemis, it would have been Artemis who would have taken revenge.

To be sure, few of us will ever find ourselves caught in the tragic role of a Phaedra or Hippolytus. But each of us is a sexual being, and each of us must practice moderation—an erotic balance between the outright denial of our sexual needs and total enslavement to our sexual desires.

Fatal Traction

Of all the women in Greek myth, Atalanta was the most athletic. She beat Achilles's vigorous father in a wrestling match and helped Meleager hunt down the savage Calydonian boar. But the best-remembered chapter in her career concerned her courtship.

Atalanta, it seems, scorned marriage because it would limit her freedom. Ever the competitor, she challenged every prospective suitor to a footrace. If he won, she would marry him; if he lost, he would die. Sometimes Atalanta would carry a spear and give the man a head start; when she crossed the finish line first, she would turn and kill him herself.

Despite the danger she posed, the challenge she presented attracted many a suitor. The man who finally won her hand was Hippomenes. As was often the case, Atalanta gave Hippomenes a head start. But Hippomenes was wily, and carried three golden apples given to him by the goddess of love. As he ran, he dropped one apple after the other, and Atalanta stopped each time to pick up each apple. The delay cost her the race and her freedom. Rejecting one temptation (sex) she was tripped up by another (the love of luxury), and love triumphed.

Prisoners of Love

One of the most powerful of human emotions is erotic love. Of all the emotions, it was the only one the Greeks called a god. Her name was Aphrodite, goddess of love. Of course, she still lives today, and we are still subject to her powers. Indeed, one of the greatest tests of moderation is the degree to which we let her rule our lives.

It is, therefore, no accident that the Greeks saw the hand of Aphrodite at work in shaping their mythic past. The multitude of their myths concerned with love teach us about the humanness and passion of the Greeks as well our own human vulnerability.

The Powers of Aphrodite

Like so many Greek myths, the legend of the Trojan War begins with a love story. Peleus, a Greek king, fell in love with Thetis, a sea nymph, and wanted to marry her. The problem was they came from two different worlds: the world of mortals and the world of the gods. To mix these two worlds was like mixing two volatile chemicals—a potentially dangerous experiment. But like so many other lovers, they believed love conquers all. So they began to plan their wedding. And to make sure it was a happy affair, they were careful to exclude from the invitation list one goddess in particular, Eris, the goddess of trouble. True to her nature, though, she came anyway, showing up at Peleus's palace with a special wedding gift, a golden apple inscribed with the words, "To the fairest." She dropped the apple at the feet of three goddesses who were standing at the reception: Hera, the queen of the gods; Athena, the goddess of wisdom; and Aphrodite, goddess of love. Of course, each bent down to pick it up, thinking—from the inscription—that it was meant for her. The three soon started to squabble, and were invited to take their dispute outside.

To resolve the issue, they chose arbitration, and went to the top of Olympus to put their case before Zeus. Zeus had a problem. If he chose Hera, his wife, as the winner of the cosmic beauty contest, he would estrange the other two goddesses; however, if he *didn't* choose Hera, his home life would be miserable. So he decided to pass the buck, and sent the three goddesses off to another mountain, Mt. Ida on the Turkish coast near Troy, where a shepherd was tending his flock. "Ask *him* to decide," Zeus said, "I'm sure he'll be an impartial judge."

And so the three goddesses flew to Mt. Ida and put their case before the young shepherd, whose name was Paris. They were not above trying to bribe the judge, however. Hera came up and offered—as queen of the gods—to make Paris the earth's most powerful king. Athena came up, and offered—as the goddess of wisdom—to make him the world's wisest philosopher. Finally, Aphrodite came up and whispered in his ear that if he chose *her* as the most beautiful goddess, she would give him the hand (and more) of the most beautiful woman on earth. True to his sensual nature, Paris chose Aphrodite.

Years later, Paris was selected to head a diplomatic mission to the Greek city of Sparta, for Paris was no ordinary shepherd but a member of Troy's royal family. Arriving at the palace of Menelaus in Sparta he found the king away on business of his own, but was hospitably received by Menelaus's wife, Queen Helen.

It was then that Aphrodite decided to cast her spell and fulfill her pledge. Helen was universally acknowledged as the most beautiful woman in all of Greece. In fact, so concerned had her father been when she was being courted that he made all her suitors swear a solemn oath: once she had made her choice and married, they would all rally together and return her to her chosen husband if any other man took her away. Of course, when Helen saw Paris, she immediately fell in love with him, and he with her. The two then made plans to sail away to Troy together, Helen abandoning her homeland, her husband, and her young daughter all for love.

When Menelaus returned home, he discovered that his wife was gone and learned the rest. Enraged at this insult to his honor, he turned for help to his big brother, Agamemnon, who was the king of the neighboring city of Mycenae and the most powerful ruler in feudal Greece. Agamemnon, in turn, saw an opportunity—not only to retrieve Helen and restore his brother's honor, but to use the incident as the pretext for making war against Troy, one of the richest cities of that time. The other kings and princes of Greece responded, not only because Agamemnon reminded them of their prior oath, but because they too saw an opportunity for increasing their wealth through plunder.

And so the Trojan War began, with a fleet of one thousand Greek ships manned by fifty thousand men. The war would drag on for ten years, for Troy had its own allies and was stoutly fortified.

What of Helen? Eventually, the Greeks won and Menelaus brought her back home. In *The Iliad*, the poet Homer introduces her to us and gives us insight into her character. She was still the prisoner of Aphrodite, but was filled with self-hate, loathing herself for yielding to desire and abandoning her child, her husband, and her home, and causing death and suffering to the people of Troy. Her name would forever more live on in infamy not as Helen of Sparta, but Helen of Troy, "the face that launched a thousand ships."

Should Aphrodite's allurements, then, be rejected because of the dangers they imply? Love *does* conquer all, but—as the ancients realized—it is *us* it conquers, for nothing can stand in its way. Sex is a life force that seeks to perpetuate the race, a force that views the individual only as an instrument of its immense power. Should sex, then, be despised? The tragic experience of Hippolytus teaches us otherwise. It is the middle, not the extremes, that we should seek. Asceticism was not the ancient Greek way. As the poet Mimnermus once wrote, "What is life if golden Aphrodite is gone?" So we should love, then, but in moderation—that is, if we can!

Even Aphrodite herself once became a prisoner of love. The Olympian gods, it seems, resented the emotional control she had over them, and none more than Zeus, whose love affairs were legion. So the king of the gods decided to give Aphrodite a taste of her own medicine by making *her* fall in love. And to make the experience as humiliating as possible, he made her fall in love with a lowly mortal. Well, not exactly lowly—Anchises was a member of Troy's royal family in the days before the war. They mated, the story goes, only once, but once was enough. Aphrodite became pregnant, eventually giving birth to a son. As for Anchises, her lover in that one-night stand, he was crippled thereafter—according to some, because he boasted of having slept with the love goddess, according to others, because the experience itself had been so intense.

Aphrodite and Helen were not the only prisoners of love. Greek myths tell of others who walked the exquisite line between pleasure and pain and by that exercise experienced love's extremes.

Pygmalion and Galatea

When we are lonely and need someone to love and someone to be loved by, our erotic imagination may construct an image of the type of person we hope to find, someone who will perfectly answer our needs, answering them in ways others have not. Of course, real life will never supply us with such perfection; how could it when we are not perfect ourselves? But if the canteen is dry, the thirsting sojourner in the desert will long to find an oasis over the next sand dune until that very longing makes water palpable.

So it was for a man named Pygmalion, who lived on the island of Cyprus. Cyprus was one of the first islands that Aphrodite visited after she was born at sea, so the island had historic connections with the erotic. According to one tradition, Pygmalion was the island's king, according to another, a sculptor. But whether sculptor or king, Pygmalion had not found the kind of woman he could give his heart to. Another of the island's traditions was prostitution, and, disgusted by the promiscuousness of Cypriote women, Pygmalion had elected to live alone. Nevertheless, in the midst of his loneliness, he continued to thirst, like a parched sailor who cannot drink the salt water that surrounds him.

One afternoon, as Pygmalion was going about his work crafting a new statue, he felt his hands moving with unconscious passion. Carving each piece of ivory with unaccustomed intensity, he attached one after the other to the matrix of wood. Taking shape in his hands, a life-sized figure began to emerge, a figure of unexpected beauty with pure skin and a gentle smile upon her lips. He tinted the lips pink and cemented in the inlaid eyes. As he did, she looked at him—or so it seemed to him—with loving gratitude. He stepped back now, admiring not his work, for she no longer seemed to be something he had created, but someone he had helped bring to life, a whole invitingly more than the sum of its parts, a perfectly beautiful female who fulfilled his every desire and expectation. Pygmalion went to take a drink of wine and returned to the statue. She seemed to be waiting for him, and he almost apologized for his brief absence.

At night he lay in bed alone, remembering the ivory face his hands touched. He could not sleep, and so he got up and went back to his studio. There she stood, the light of the moon palely reflected on her naked skin. He sat down beside her and looked up into her face. "If only you were real," he thought.

[51]

The next morning he woke up on the floor of his studio, where he had fallen asleep. In the glaring light of the sun, the statue he had sculpted now seemed just a statue and nothing more, beautiful on the surface but with no spirit within.

That night he again lay alone. From outside his window, he could hear the laughter of a couple walking down the street. He followed their voices until the two turned the corner and the sound faded away. As he lay there restlessly, he thought of a poem written by another island lover, Sappho:

> Down has gone the moon,
> and Pleiades, half-gone is
> night, time passes,
> and I lie alone.

But for Pygmalion, the moon had not yet set. He got up and walked into the studio again. She was still standing there, illuminated in the moonlight, silently radiant and pure. It was then that he did something quite extraordinary, something that revealed the extremity of his longing and his hopelessness. Gently, he lifted the statue up and took it to bed, laying its head down on the pillow beside him. Placing his hand on her chest, he stroked the smooth breasts he had sculpted from ivory, and pressed his lips against her ivory cheek, uttering her name for the first time, "Galatea," he called her, a name that meant "milk-white." As she glistened in the moonlight, he continued to speak to her, telling her how much he loved her and how long he had waited for her to come into his life.

In the morning he put the statue back on its pedestal, this time draping the body in a diaphanous wrap he had bought the day before in the marketplace. Next he placed a screen in front of her so no one else could see the masterpiece he had fashioned. At night he once again brought her to his bed, undressing her and embracing her until he drifted into sleep.

The following day was the festival of Aphrodite, the island's most joyous holiday. Going to the goddess's temple, Pygmalion prayed to her from the depths of his heart, "Let the woman I love be alive, and let her love me with a love equal to my own." In his mind he knew the prayer was impossible to answer. Better to pray to Aesclepius, the god of healing, to cure his madness and end his self-deception, but that very madness and self-deception filled his soul as nothing else had ever done, and therefore he could not utter the prayer.

In the evening Pygmalion observed what had by now become a ritual, taking Galatea to bed and lying beside her until morning. But this night as he lay his arm across her chest, her ivory breasts felt soft and warm, and rose and fell as the statue—yes!—breathed. Its eyes, which had always been open until then, blinked, and from them tears rolled down. "Galatea," he said, amazed. "Galatea."

Her name was all he could speak as she turned to him and kissed him, and spoke his name as though she had known him from the day of her birth, which, in truth, she had. Aphrodite, for whom all things are possible, had answered Pygmalion's prayer in recognition of his longing.

Some say the story of Pygmalion and Galatea describes our nature as human beings. To be human, they say, is to be incomplete. Our lives, they say, are a constant search for completion, which we achieve in flesh and in spirit by embracing another who turns to us even as we turn to him or her to make us whole. We were made male and female by the gods, but as individuals we are aching halves that must find each other.

The universe, the philosopher Pythagoras taught, was composed of such opposites, of extremes: day and night, light and darkness, odd and even, woman and man. Only in the mystic union of these opposites, only in their joining, could the cosmos be comprehended.

Others say the story is not about the attraction we feel for each other, but our longing for beauty and its perfection, a compulsion that artists like Pygmalion know intimately. Inevitably it is a perfection that lies beyond anyone's reach. Even Galatea, from the very moment she awoke, began to age. In that very moment began her beauty's decline, for all things that are alive must degenerate as they travel the long road from the extreme of birth to that of death. Pygmalion would learn that truth each day as he looked into Galatea's face and contemplated her once-ivory body. But such decay is a concomitant of life. Only he who is content with a lifeless work of art will reject a real woman; but he who accepts a real woman will never own the ideal.

Such an ideal can only be captured in art. It is the precious moment caught in a single frame of film, but let the film go on and one moment lapses into another. Like sand, moonlight slips through our fingers.

It is such agonizing perfection that English poet John Keats wrote of in his "Ode on a Grecian Urn"—agonizing because it tortures us with a consummate and unchanging beauty that can never be possessed in life.

> Bold lover, never, never canst thou kiss,
> Though winning near the goal – yet, do not grieve;
> She cannot fade, though thou hast not thy bliss,
> For ever wilt thou love, and she be fair!

Such perfection, never cloyed, belongs to art, not to real life. Yet, as Keats noted, such perfection shows us the goal we must aspire toward, those evanescent moments that make all the rest of life worthwhile.

The quest for perfection can cause us intense pain, the kind of pain Pygmalion knew. If we moderate our desires and expectations, we can spare ourselves needless suffering.

Tortured by a vision of perfect beauty and agonized by the realization of its impermanence, the artists of ancient Greece sought to "freeze-frame" such beauty using the media that they had at their disposal. Denied the video camera, they used the painter's brush and the sculptor's chisel. On their vases and in their statues, their classical vision of beauty endures.

Once we understand and accept that life is only fleeting moments, that it cannot be owned or possessed, we realize how precious life really is. In the end, Galatea the statue, however perfect, would have ceased to gratify Pygmalion. Her silence would have ceased to answer his need. Only her living voice and thoughts would have satisfied his hunger.

That is not to say Pygmalion the perfectionist would always have been pleased by everything the human Galatea would have said! In giving the statue life, Aphrodite also gave Galatea freedom and independence. Her freedom and independence were a price Pygmalion would have to pay.

It is the same lesson Professor Henry Higgins had to learn in George Bernard Shaw's play *Pygmalion*, which inspired the later Broadway musical, *My Fair Lady*.

A much earlier playwright, William Shakespeare, based his play *Romeo and Juliet* on another Greek myth about love and its price, and it is to that myth we now turn.

Pyramus and Thisbe

We often associate the emotional extremes of love with impassioned youth, and so it is in the myth of Pyramus and Thisbe. Set in ancient Babylon, the story concerns two lovers—a boy named Pyramus and a girl named Thisbe—who lived in neighboring houses that shared a common wall. Their parents had discouraged their friendship, but there was a chink in the wall, and through it the two lovers would speak, sharing their feelings and hopes.

Eventually, the two grew bolder and planned a tryst. They would leave their houses separately and meet at the tomb of King Ninus at the city's edge. Thisbe got there first and waited beside the tomb for Pyramus's arrival. Hearing a lion's roar, she hid in fear in a nearby cave, dropping her scarf as she ran. Sure enough, the lion came by, fresh from the kill and dripping with gore. Spying the scarf, he snatched it up and shook it and shredded it in his bloody jaws.

A while later, Pyramus came by. Calling out Thisbe's name and seeing her nowhere in sight, he circled the tomb and saw the mangled and bloody scarf. Horrified and convinced that Thisbe had been mauled to death by a lion, Pyramus drew his sword and plunged it into his chest, preferring to kill himself rather than live without the girl he loved. As for Thisbe, she soon returned to the site of the tomb. Seeing Pyramus's lifeless body on the ground beside his sword, and the blood-stained scarf at a distance, she realized what must have ensued. Rather than living alone, she too determined to follow the boy she loved into death. Taking Pyramus's sword into her hands, she fell on its blade to join her beloved in Hades's realm.

Before her suicide, Thisbe prayed that their parents would forgive them and bury them together there in the same tomb. She also prayed to the gods that the nearby tree would shade their common grave and become a memorial to their undying love. Thisbe's prayer was answered. Her ashes and Pyramus's were deposited in the same urn, and the urn was buried beside the mulberry tree. From that time forward the tree turned blood red as its berries ripened in miraculous commemoration of the lovers' tragic death. To be young is to be impulsive, to live a life of extremes. To be young and in love can invite pain, even tragedy.

While it may be unrealistic to expect young lovers to practice moderation, the story of Pyramus and Thisbe reveals the risks in ignoring it. But their story was told with compassion, for the two exemplified one of life's noblest instincts, the instinct to love.

At the other end of life's spectrum from youth is old age. But aging does not extinguish the fires of love, which still glow in the embers of the heart. The matching "bookend" to the tale of Pyramus and Thisbe is our next myth, the tale of two elderly lovers, Baucis and Philemon.

The Rewards of Kindness

The story of Baucis and Philemon is set in the land of Phrygia, a kingdom contained in the country today known as Turkey. As the story goes, Zeus and Hermes were traveling across country, not as gods, but in disguise as ordinary human beings. Seeking shelter for the night, they knocked on one door after another, but no one was generous enough to offer them hospitality. Finally, the two gods came to a humble cottage where an elderly couple lived. When the gods knocked on the door, they were given welcome and offered a simple dinner, the best the couple could provide from their resources.

After dinner, the gods revealed their true identity, much to the old couple's astonishment. "Come with us," the gods said, "Let's climb up the mountain." When the four of them reached the mountaintop, the elderly husband and wife—Philemon, the husband, and Baucis, the wife—turned around to look back. What they saw shocked them. The entire countryside was flooded and all their neighbors' homes drowned, all except their own. Only their cottage was no longer a cottage anymore, but had been transformed into a glorious temple adorned with marble columns and a golden roof. "We have punished your miserly neighbors, and now we want to reward you," said Zeus. "Ask us any favor, and we will grant it."

Baucis and Philemon looked at each other and spoke together for a while, and then addressed the gods with a modest request. "May we be the priest and priestess of your temple? And, since we have known and loved each other all our lives, please also grant that neither of us will have to see the other die first and survive in loneliness as widower or widow." "So be it," said Zeus, and Baucis and Philemon returned to the valley to serve the gods' temple. Many years later, as they stood before its doors, each was miraculously transformed into a tree, a leafy oak and a leafy linden entwined. The two trees were thereafter revered by the people of the countryside as living symbols of piety and abiding love.

This story is not a celebration of poverty (Baucis and Philemon led humble lives, but were not destitute) nor is it the corollary, a condemnation of wealth (the temple was roofed in gold). Instead, the myth teaches that goodness is not to be measured on an economic scale. The virtue of Baucis and Philemon was the virtue of generosity, of giving what they were capable of giving. And the favor they asked of the gods was not a materialistic one, but one defined by affection for each other and service to the gods. Their wish was modest, their reward divine.

The Myth of Aging

Most Greek art focused not on the very young or the very old, but on the time in between those extremes. Greek writers and artists were not so much interested in the rose as a bud or as an aggregate of withering petals, but as a flower in full bloom. It was that full bloom that best expressed the rose's essence and its perfection, and the essential and the perfect were perpetual preoccupations of the Greek mind.

As for old age itself, it was spoken of as merciless and remorseless, with burdens to bear heavier than the weight of Mt. Aetna. The Greeks resented not just the infirmities of old age, but also the aesthetic damage it did to the body. The physical deterioration caused by aging grated on those Hellenistic sensibilities that prized beauty in all things. For this reason, few old people are depicted in classical Greek art. Instead, what we see are the physiques of those who are vitally mature and vigorous, not decrepit and weak. If the Greek word *kalós* meant "good," as well as "beautiful," its opposite *aischrós* meant "shameful," as well as "ugly." Ugliness, in short, was something to be ashamed of, and accordingly aging was a curse, at least in the eyes of the classical period, or fifth century B.C.

But as the classical period comes to a close, we begin to hear a voice of rebuttal that builds to a defiant roar. Rejecting the sanitizing tendencies of classical art, the sculptors of the post-classical age decided to give the elderly their due as deserving life-members of the human race. As a result, statues of the fourth century B.C. and Hellenistic Age depict them with heroic dignity and stark realism. For its part, late Greek poetry attests to the passions that persist in the soul despite the outward debilitation of the body. Growing old and tasting the bitterness of the ashes, the late erotic poets of Greece chose to live in verse as the flame. "Desire is stronger than time," wrote one. "In my hungry heart," penned another, "the embers still burn." Declared another, "Not yet shall we cease from the Muses who called us to the dance." To paraphrase, "If we must die, then let us die dancing!"

What these statues and poems teach us is that being old means living at the edge. If old age is an extreme, then this is one extreme we must embrace. In defiance of Apollo's dictum, we must live out our days in spirited excess, for those are the only days we will have left. If there ever was a prime directive in Greek thought that overrode all others, it was the passion for life, and when the end of life is near, the need for passion becomes all the greater even in the face of moderation's rebuke.

A young Achilles could surrender his life for undying fame. But that was his *choice*. Dying from old age is *not* our choice, but if we must grow old, then we should do it heroically, calling upon all of our remaining powers in a final effort to validate our existence.

The model here is Ulysses, not Homer's Ulysses, but Tennyson's, the Ithacan senior citizen who tears up his AARP card and decides instead to live undefeated and undiscounted in one last great adventure of the human spirit. Or Philemon and Baucis, who served and stood, rooted as trees to the ground they had grown on and loved. Or Laertes, Ulysses's aged father, who in the *The Odyssey's* final act became the first to hurl his spear at the enemy.

Prisoners of Matter

Just as erotic desire draws us to one another, so does the desire for material possessions draw us to things. Both impulses stem from the same human need: the need to be more than we are, a need that is satisfied not by internal growth but by external acquisition.

But just as carnal desire can sometimes end by hurting us, so can the appetite for material possessions. The Stoic philosophers of Greece argued that we do not own our possessions as much as we are owned by them. In effect, the more things we own, the greater their claim upon us. Own one house and you will eventually need to make household repairs; own two houses and your problems will be doubled. Thus the person who is most truly free is, ironically, the one who has the least.

There are many Greek myths that describe the price we can pay for loving another human being. Ariadne and Medea were betrayed by the men they loved, and Helen of Troy sacrificed her honor. But there are other myths that describe the price we can pay for loving *things* too much. Midas, for example, quickly learned to rue his golden touch. Our love of people and our love of things can each be carried to excess, and each can cause suffering and tragedy.

The Legend of Atlantis

Suffering and tragedy can occur on a massive scale if greed characterizes an entire society. In two of his philosophical dialogues, the *Timaeus* and *Critias*, Plato tells how avarice once destroyed a whole civilization. According to Plato's account, the story was first reported by an Athenian scholar named Solon, who visited Egypt in the sixth century B.C. and heard the tale from an Egyptian priest.

Once upon a time, as the story goes, there existed a rich and powerful island civilization, so vast that it was set in the ocean on whose far shore Atlas held up the heavens. The ocean was accordingly named the Atlantic, and the civilization, Atlantis. The people of Atlantis worshiped bulls and the god of the sea, and they were great seafarers whose influence reached to the shores of the Mediterranean as far as Egypt and Greece. Their culture was highly advanced for its time: they were literate and skilled in the arts of metallurgy and architecture. Yet despite their wealth, they always wanted more, and their greed turned them into arrogant imperialists who dreamed of dominating Europe and the Near East. In the end it was this extremism that destroyed them.

Their divine patience exhausted, the gods decided to punish the people for their hubris. Accordingly, the waters of the ocean rose in a great surge, and in one terrible day and night the civilization of Atlantis disappeared beneath the sea, never again to surface.

The legend of the lost kingdom of Atlantis contains a core of moral and historic truth: nations are frequently destroyed by their expansionist aims. King Croesus of Lydia learned this lesson to his regret when he invaded the territory of the Persians. Plato's own city of Athens was destroyed by its imperialistic ambitions. Affluence inspires arrogance, arrogance engenders folly, and folly invites nemesis. It does not matter whether or not a nation believes in the gods of the Greeks. The cosmic consequences remain the same. The same universal law applies to all: exceed your proper limits, reject moderation, and you will be taught your proper size. It is a lesson all dictators, ancient and modern, have been compelled to learn, but sadly new tyrants always arise who haven't gone to school.

The Trojan War

To save a stolen queen named Helen, the Greeks launched an armada of a thousand ships and laid siege to Troy's mighty citadel, only to be stymied for ten years. In the end, they won not by strength, but by deception, with the cunning Trojan Horse, filled with commandos, that gained entry to the walled city. Troy was subsequently looted and burned, and the Greeks sailed home with their golden plunder.

Chief among the cities of Greece then was Mycenae, home of Agamemnon, commander-in-chief of the Greek army that had fought at Troy. From the name of that city, then the wealthiest and strongest of Greece, comes the name "Mycenaean" used to describe Greeks of that heroic age. But for all Mycenae's stout fortifications, it and the other citadels of the Mycenaean world were destroyed some two centuries after Troy's own demise. Afterward, Greece devolved into a period of Dark Ages that lasted for some four centuries.

Who had destroyed the fortresses of the Mycenaeans? And, even more significantly, by what means had the enemy achieved their objective? The Greeks themselves believed that the cause of the destruction was an invasion from the north by a wave of new Greek immigrants. But what had allowed them to be triumphant over such a powerful enemy, the warrior race that had once captured Troy? Scholars do not have that answer. The Mycenaean Greeks may have been worn out by the long war against Troy. They may have been weakened by internecine warfare that followed their return from abroad. There may have been other causes too, such as famine or disease. But whatever the reason or combination of reasons, their giant-sized walls proved an inadequate defense against their new opponents. They who had lived by the sword died by the sword, and the greed that had led them to Troy became the same greed that motivated their own destroyers.

It was during the Dark Ages of Greece that the heroic poems of Homer were composed. *The Iliad* told of the Trojan War itself, *The Odyssey*, of the war's aftermath as one hero in particular, Ulysses, struggled to make his way back home and rebuild the pre-war society he had been forced to leave. Greed and its consequences and the tragic defiance of moderation are themes in each poem.

A Quarrel over Concubines

The Iliad begins with a battle over possessions. Forced to return a Trojan concubine to her father, Agamemnon takes Achilles's concubine in compensation, infuriating Achilles and provoking him to withdraw from the Trojan War. The argument is over women, but not over love, because these women were possessions and symbols of prestige. For nine years Agamemnon had taken the pick of the spoils of war for himself, and Achilles had resented it. The taking of Achilles's concubine became the last straw. In the end, a war that had been fought over the ownership of a woman, Helen, ended with a battle over two other female status symbols. In consequence, even more blood was spilled.

Greed in The Odyssey

On their homeward way, Ulysses and his men landed at an island ruled by a king named Aeolus, who was charged by the gods with the responsibility of controlling the winds. After hospitably receiving Ulysses, Aeolus sent the Greek hero on his way with a favorable wind to speed his voyage. Aeolus also gave Ulysses a special gift, which he enclosed in a tightly bound leather bag.

Once under sail, weary Ulysses fell asleep. But the members of his crew were awake, and wondered what the bag contained. Perhaps it was silver; perhaps it was gold. So while their captain was sleeping, they decided to satisfy their curiosity and avarice by untying the bag and looking inside.

The moment the bag was loosened, the "gift" rushed out. Aeolus had given Ulysses a bag of winds. With the release of the winds, a violent storm ensued that almost sank the ship before blowing it back to Aeolus's island. Upset that his gift had been misused, Aeolus angrily sent Ulysses on his way, but without any wind to help him cross the vastness of the sea. The greed of his foolish men had cost Ulysses an easy passage home.

Ten years would pass before Ulysses finally arrived home in Ithaca. Even then a battle awaited him, for during his absence his palace had been occupied by the arrogant nobles of his kingdom who plotted the murder of Prince Telemachus, Ulysses's son, butchered his herds and drank his wine, and waited for Ulysses's wife, Penelope, to choose one of them as her new husband.

Despite the fact that they were of aristocratic blood, the poet paints the suitors as the real enemies of society because they had no respect for its norms. Selfish users, they contributed nothing to their community, but only took rather than gave. In the end, Ulysses killed them all in a savage confrontation, avenging not only their crimes against the throne but their sins against civilization.

The common lesson in these two episodes is that greed can seduce men and become their undoing. Only by moderating and restraining our appetite can we survive and prosper.

The Ring of Gyges

What makes self-control so difficult is that our appetites know no bounds except those enforced by conscience and law, and conscience is shaped by the fear of punishment. Left to our own devices, and exempt from any and all punishment, our inner nature would lead us to gratify our every desire.

A cynical assessment of human nature, to be sure, which is why it is so important for us to decide how we want our lives to be lived—as creatures of base appetite, or as something more. This is the issue that Plato grappled with in his dialogue *The Republic*. To illustrate the issue, one of the participants in the dialogue narrated a story about a man named Gyges and a magical ring he found.

According to the story, Gyges discovered an underground tomb containing a corpse that wore a golden ring. Taking the ring home and putting it on his finger, he found to his amazement that when he turned the bezel of the ring toward the inside of his hand, the people around him began to speak of him as though he was no longer there. When he turned to bezel to the outside of his hand again, it was as though he had reappeared.

For Plato, this mythical ring of invisibility became a fictional test of an individual's ethical resolve. Possessed of such a ring, the philosopher asked, who could resist becoming invisible in order to satisfy his every desire? Steal, and no one would see you. Sleep with a woman, and your identity would remain unknown. Is the measure of humanity, then, no more than our basest instinct? Are we merely animals restrained by the cage of the law?

No, answered Plato, for there is an internal reason for living a righteous life. In fact, a life of self-restraint that acknowledges limits to behavior is best not only for society but also for the individual. Translated into personal terms, Plato's lesson is that each of us must strive for the Golden Mean in order to achieve harmony within ourselves because that is the only pathway to inner peace and lasting happiness.

The Republic of the Soul

In *The Republic*, Plato tried to describe the composition of an ideal state. It is for this reason that his work has been given its traditional name. But his larger and deeper purpose was to describe the composition of the ideal personality. Plato begins his work with a discussion of government because he realizes that a nation is a bigger, and therefore easier, target to aim at than one person, but his primary concern is the individual.

As the discussion develops, we see that the perfect state needs three components: able workers, brave defenders, and wise leaders. All three must collaborate and none alone can be sufficient. But of the three components, the most critical is wise leadership; without it no nation can attain its fullest potential.

Plato then points out that the three essential components of a state are analogous to three parts of the human personality. Matching the workers are our basic energies and needs, matching the defenders are our emotions and aspirations, and matching the leaders are our minds. Just as wise leaders must guide the state, so must the mind guide the life of the individual.

But also there must be balance, with each part of the human personality playing its proper role and receiving its due reward. An individual, after all, is not just a brain, or heart, or stomach. Nor are we only our thoughts, our feelings, or our appetites. A whole person is all these things working together. Should we allow our thoughts to drown out our feelings, or our appetites to crowd out our thoughts, our optimal humanity will be diminished. To live a life of moderation is to give to each part of ourselves its fair share.

The Language of Art

The balance that Plato sought for the human personality permeates the spirit of classical Greek art, for it was through art that the classical Greeks gave material expression to the intellectual values they held dear.

The Discus Thrower

One of the most famous examples is the statue *The Discus Thrower* by the Athenian sculptor Myron. More then simply personifying the athletic pursuit of excellence, the statue also embodies the virtue of moderation.

Of the infinite number of poses the sculptor could have selected to portray the act of hurling a discus, Myron chose the moment between the wind-up and the release, the moment that sums up what has gone before and points to what is yet to come, a moment in which the athlete stands poised between past and future, critically intent upon the present. At that moment—outside of time and yet within it—the discus thrower becomes one with the discus he holds, his curved and outstretched arms fusing with his bent shoulders to form an arc that forecasts the parabolic trajectory of his projectile.

Students of human kinetics claim that a discus cannot be thrown from such a pose, that a real athlete would fall down if he tried. But the sculptor ignores the limitations of physical reality to capture a spiritual ideal, the ideal of perfect equilibrium of body and mind. A contemporary athlete might talk of being "in the zone," a Zen archer, of becoming one with the bow, but it is all the same idea, though the Greeks were the first to conceive it.

Regrettably, the original statue that Myron made (of marble or, more likely, of bronze) is lost. Like most other original sculptures from the hands of the Greek masters, it was destroyed by Early Christian zeal or Dark Age ignorance. Therefore we must reconstitute Myron's ancient vision from surviving Roman copies.

Poetically speaking, this is as it should be, since absolute perfection is always out of reach, perfect equilibrium always elusive. Perhaps the Greeks did not direct us to find the middle, but instead urged us to avoid the extremes because from a practical standpoint they realized that extremes are far easier to identify than the delicate place between.

The Ludovisi Throne

Even though the original *Discus Thrower* does not exist, the original Ludovisi Throne does, though the name of its classical sculptor is lost. Whether this mysterious work was a throne at all is uncertain since it is made of stone and lacks legs. Ludovisi is simply the name of a noble Italian family that once owned it. What we know for sure is that this object was cut from a single block of marble and resembles an empty box with three vertical sides, each of which was carved in relief on the outside.

The central panel shows a woman rising from what seems to be a pool of water. The water itself is not shown but is alluded to by the wet tunic that clings to her breasts, by its ripple-like folds, and her downflowing streams of hair. Her face is turned to the left as she gazes up at another woman who is helping her climb out of the water. To the right another woman strikes a similar pose. Together they hold a cloth in which to wrap and dry her. What is this scene meant to represent?

The best theory suggests that the scene portrays the birth of Aphrodite, the goddess of erotic love. A Greek myth tells us that Aphrodite was born upon the foam of the sea; indeed, her name in Greek means "foam-born." From her marine birthplace she was wafted across the billows on a floating seashell to an island, where women helped her ashore and became her first devotees. (The Renaissance painter Botticelli depicted this vision in his *Birth of Venus*, and a Roman painting on the same subject was found in the ruins of Pompeii.) The front of the Ludovisi Throne may depict this mythic episode. On the paired wings that form the left and right panels of the Throne are two female figures, one on the left and one on the right, each in a seated pose. The figure to the right, naked and seated upon a soft pillow, plays music on a woodwind instrument; the figure to the left, heavily clothed and seated upon a hard pillow, burns incense on a stand. Together they symmetrically complement the central panel as they provide an aesthetic accompaniment to the ritual of divine birth. Combined with the center they also constitute a triptych of sensuality, a continuum that progresses from the full nakedness of the flute player to the semi-nudity of Aphrodite to the total draping of the woman burning incense. Together the three scenes may also comprise the chapters in an ancient Greek woman's sexual biography—from unwed virgin to bride to matron—if we understand the erotic ritual in the center as a preparation for marriage.

The three-part design of the Ludovisi Throne presents a holistic vision of life, one in which its separate parts combine to make a balanced whole. It is a design that would have pleased the philosopher Aristotle, who argued that every good story must have a beginning, a middle, and an end that are organically united.

As such, the design is also a prescription for a worthwhile life, one in which our beginnings and our ends are endowed with meaning by the central purpose to which we have dedicated our days. This purpose need not be marriage, but it must be *something* we have consciously chosen, something that will replace randomness with vital direction.

To help us find that direction, the Greeks have given us a compass of sorts. It does not point to an arbitrary north, for it is a humanistic compass that recognizes that we must each find our own way. What it *does* tell us is to avoid extremes, because by avoiding them we may find the one path that for us is golden, a path that is peaceful and secure, where the air is fragrant with incense, the flute plays, and Aphrodite rises from the sea.

The balanced composition found in the Ludovisi Throne occurs elsewhere in Greek sculpture, in particular among the statues used to decorate temples. At each end of a Greek temple, high above its columns, was a triangular section called a pediment formed by the sloping sides of the roof. As a people passionately in love with life, the ancient Greeks couldn't bear the thought of building a structure from which life was absent. So they decorated the exteriors of their temples with semblances of life, carved from marble so they would endure.

Among the architectural parts they adorned were the pediments. These they filled with three-dimensional statues that stood on the pediment floor. Each set of statues told a story from mythology about the Greeks' heroes and gods. Because each pediment was a triangle, the sculptural panorama had to conform to its shape: a sculptor could place his tallest figure(s) in the middle (under the apex), but had to gradually reduce the heights of his other figures (by having them kneel or recline) as he approached the two ends. The result was a symmetrical design in which the central statue was framed by matching pairs of subordinate ones at the pediment's extremities.

Other forms of ancient Greek art are resplendent in such symmetry.

Out of practical necessity every Greek vase or wine cup was structurally balanced, but this fundamental structure was augmented by twin handles and a painted decoration that highlighted the underlying symmetry (with one seated or standing warrior, for example, painted opposite another).

Coins, too, embodied symmetry. Indeed, it is no accident that the Greeks were the first people in the history of the world to invent coins that were decorated on both sides. To their way of thinking, the two-sidedness of a coin cried out for designs on both sides and, furthermore, designs that matched. The Athenians, for instance, were the first to come up with the idea of a coin literally with heads on one side and tails on the other: Athena's face in profile on the front, and her pet, the wise old owl, on the back.

This penchant for symmetry and balance in Greek art may have been an outgrowth of their humanism; recognizing on an abstract level that the human body is bilaterally symmetrical, they decided to remake the world in the image of woman and man. By populating their man-made environment with symmetrical works, they reinforced the prominence of symmetry in their mind's eye.

Keeping things in balance was thus a dictum not only of Greek ethics but also of Greek aesthetics. Fittingly, the ancient Greek word for morally good—*kalós*—was also the word for beautiful. What was beautiful was good, and what was good was beautiful. As the philosopher Plotinus once said, "In visible things and in all else, what is beautiful is patterned." As artists who shape our lives, we too must strive for balance, searching (as a digital Plotinus might say) for the pattern in the noise.

The Art of Language

"The Greeks have a word for it." So the saying goes, and so they did, with a nuanced language tailored to the keenness of their thoughts. Many of their words have entered our own language, as much because of what the

Greeks thought as what they said—whole subjects like history, drama, and psychology, along with the words to name them.

Two of their words that have not entered our language are *men* and *de*, but they inform us about the Greek mind as few other words can. *Men* is best translated as "on the one hand," *de* as "on the other hand," and they function as a pair. Thus an ancient Greek might say, "On one hand (*men*), this man speaks eloquently, but on the other hand (*de*), what he says isn't true." The fact that the Greeks used *men* and *de* frequently is instructive because it shows us they viewed reality not through one eye only but through both eyes at once. They looked at things from both sides (which may explain why they enjoyed debating so much), and therefore saw things in depth and with perspective.

In a way, *men* and *de* represent extremes, and imply that the truth may lie somewhere in between. Even if not, the mere act of simultaneously holding two diametrically opposed ideas in one's head can sharpen one's mental acuity like nothing else. Indeed, out of the dynamic tension between such opposites can come a third and better way.

Question and answer, challenge and response, was the verbal and mental technique that Socrates and Plato used to find the truth, carefully honing the definitions of things by rubbing one opposing idea against another. Likewise in Athenian jury trials, after a verdict of guilty had come down, it was customary to ask both the defendant and his accuser to propose alternative sentences. Knowing that the jury would be prone to reject too harsh a penalty, the accuser would be induced to be more lenient toward his enemy; knowing the jury would be prone to reject too light a penalty, the defendant would be induced to be harder on himself. And thus the jury would be given two relatively moderate sentences to choose between.

The principles of opposition and balance also determined the structural style of Greek literature. Almost every Greek literary work was based on an invisible architectural plan. In such a plan the chief principle of design was symmetry. Elements at the beginning of a story corresponded to elements at the end by analogy or contrast, forming a series of concentric frames that enclosed a narrative centerpiece.

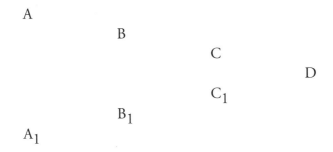

The amazing thing is that these patterns only become visible if a work is looked at under a literary microscope, and therefore many patterns were not discovered by modern scholars until the twentieth century. Indeed, some still lie hidden, awaiting the scrutiny of future classicists.

Of course, the Greeks did not create such patterns to be obscure and mysterious; they created them because they wanted to create works of beauty, and to their minds what was beautiful was patterned. To create a work of art in images or words meant to summon order out of chaos using the power of the mind. In the Greek language, the word *kósmos* meant "order," but it also meant "beauty." Thus beauty and order were synonymous: what was beautiful had to be orderly and what was orderly must be beautiful. (The notion of order survives in our word *cosmos*, and the notion of beauty in our word *cosmetics*.) The mythological poet Hesiod tells us that Chaos existed first, and only later did Earth come into being.

What all of this can suggest to us is the potential value of order in our lives, a commodity so rare in these hectic times that we may lose sight of its bearing on our happiness. To create a beautiful life for ourselves and those we love may require a conscious effort, greater than we have yet made, to build a framework of order within which love and creativity can flourish, and without which they cannot thrive.

That doesn't mean we have to speak in symmetrical sentences. But it does mean we have to think clearly and precisely enough to define our priorities. We may begin to see these priorities for the first time only when we have banished from our day-to-day lives the excesses of our times.

Dangerous Curve Ahead

At this point in our discussion we need to confront a popular misconception: all the ancient Greeks were philosophers, and they all walked around being philosophical. First of all, they weren't all philosophers. There were a lot of farmers and fishermen and politicians, and a lot of them probably never thought too deeply about anything except maybe making ends meet and, if possible, getting ahead. It can be misleading, however, to talk about philosophers in a professional sense (though they did eventually arise in Greek society). What should concern us instead is a certain philosophical turn of mind that looked at things more deeply than their surface showed and cared deeply about knowing the inner truth. In that respect, the ancient Greeks, especially the Athenians, were philosophers indeed.

Did they walk around philosophizing all the time? Not likely. Here especially, the "practice of moderation" may mislead us. No nation, no people, that is moderate needs constantly to remind itself to be moderate. Only those who are prone to excess, and have frequently paid the price for it, need be reminded. Similarly, we're not likely to spot a sign that says "Dangerous Curve Ahead!" on an interminable stretch of straight highway. Such signs are only put up where danger is at hand. The Greeks were, and are, a passionate people. If they weren't, they would never have written tragedies in which they were the subjects. Or gone to war so often. Or loved freedom so much. Or, lastly, have been so interesting to study. No, they were not bloodless philosophers; they were human beings like ourselves.

Practicing Moderation

In evolutionary terms, emotion preceded intellect. Therefore, if we're human, going to extremes comes easy. If moderation means observing the Golden Mean, how do we find the Mean in the first place? The Greeks tell us: first find the extremes; once you find the extremes, it's easy to find the middle. In effect, what works for measuring a wall or a piece of paper can work for gauging behavior.

Once again we need an inventory, but this time an even more personal one. Stop and reflect. What do you do too much of? Eat? Drink? Work? Where do you overdo it, hurting yourself and others in the process?

Unfortunately, the extremist life isn't so easy to identify. When we're living it, we're so "carried away" that we're too far away to see where we've gone wrong.

Compared to a life of exciting excess, practicing moderation may seem dreadfully dull. But the ancient Greeks weren't trying to sell a life of boredom. All they were doing was warning us that if we go too far in one direction, we may pay a high price. Even the pursuit of excellence, they warned, can become dangerous if carried too far.

But for emotional beings like us, moderation goes against the grain. Instead of steady common sense, we prefer the quick fix. Take health, for example. How should a person maintain a healthy body? By moderate exercise and moderate eating, including a sensibly balanced diet. With consistent effort, barring accident, a healthy body should result. But the recipe is too unappealing to our psychological appetite. Yet how else, but by moderation, could one succeed over the long-term? Nevertheless, a book based on such a dull principle would barely sell, since Americans are more fixated on rapid weight loss than long-term health.

Moderation may not make you thin, but it can make you healthy. It can save you from a life of emotional bingeing and a life of emotional guilt. Moderation may not make you rich, but it can make you secure. If you dabble in stocks and bonds, the dullest style of investing is diversification, yet it is also the safest. Diversification means building a balanced portfolio based on the premise that what is doing well today may not do well tomorrow, and vice versa. Spreading your bets reduces your risk. But as every savvy investor knows, the greatest profits involve the greatest risks. If the ancient Greeks had had a stock market, they might have bet on some hot stocks occasionally (they were, after all, a race of risk takers), but they were also intimately familiar with the danger of losing everything. Moderation, then, in all things, including, perhaps, moderation itself!

Moderation vs. Excellence

By now, however, you may have detected what may appear as a glaring contradiction in my argument. How can someone practice moderation, you may ask, at the very time they're pursuing excellence? Pursuing excellence means pushing things to the limit; practicing moderation means holding back. Aren't the two principles, then, contradictory?

The simple answer is yes. The real answer is more complicated.

To begin with, civilizations can often be defined by the coexistence of opposing principles. It is the static electricity crackling between the poles that defines a civilization's unique character. Take Roman civilization, for example: how can a culture that was committed to the making of law tolerate the butchery of the Colosseum? The answer is that each act was a function of power. Take America: how can a nation dedicated to the pursuit of happiness debauch itself in materialism? The answer is that each attitude is a function of freedom. The concepts of power and freedom thus reconcile the seemingly contradictory aspects of their respective cultures. And so the pursuit of excellence (pillar No. 2) and the practice of moderation (pillar No. 3) can stand side by side in the temple of Greek culture. Each is reconciled with the other by the humanistic nature of Greek thought, which viewed the reduction of risks as a necessary component of self-realization.

The two principles, then, excellence and moderation, are not simply contradictory; they are, in fact, also complementary. Consider the automobile you drive. On the floorboard is the accelerator and a brake pedal. One makes you go fast, the other slows you down, but to have a real car you need both. In terms of Greek civilization, the gas pedal is the pursuit of excellence; the brake pedal is the practice of moderation. Just as we need both to drive a car, so the ancient Greeks needed both to run their civilization. And so might we need both to lead productive lives.

I'm sure you wouldn't want to buy a car that had a fast engine but no brakes. It just wouldn't be safe. But by the same token, you wouldn't want a car that had perfect brakes but no engine. That wouldn't be any fun at all, and it certainly wouldn't get you anywhere.

In my hearts of hearts, I suspect if the ancient Greeks had had to choose between those two vehicles, they would have taken the one with no brakes. Dangerous, yes, but what a ride! Far better than sitting in the garage and going nowhere.

In the end, then, the best illustration of the need for moderation is not a calorie counter or the Dow Jones average, but the lowly floorboard of our automobile. A gas pedal and a set of brakes: the pursuit of excellence and the practice of moderation. Both are needed for safe driving, and a person would be a fool to ignore their proper use. But how do you know when to step on the gas, and when to apply the brakes? In short, how do you become a good "driver" of your life? The answer is contained in our next principle.

CHAPTER 4

THE FOURTH PILLAR
SELF-KNOWLEDGE

The fourth pillar of Greek wisdom is self-knowledge. Self-knowledge is needed in order to choose wisely between the pursuit of excellence and the practice of moderation. Only through an assessment of our personal strengths and weaknesses can we know when it is time to press boldly ahead or pull back. It is for this reason that this principle was the second to be carved over the entranceway to Apollo's temple at Delphi. There for all to read were the words *Gnóthi seautón,* "Know thyself."

The Oracle at Delphi

The site of the temple at Delphi, about seventy-five miles northwest of Athens, is one of the most dramatic in all Greece. The temple sits beneath a towering mountain on the shoulder of a ravine that plunges into a deep gorge filled with a broad river of olive trees that pours out to the sea.

It was at Delphi that the god Apollo slew a serpentine monster called the Python, and there a temple was built to commemorate his victory. Because Apollo was a god of prophecy, the priestess who dwelt in his temple foretold the future. After chewing sacred laurel leaves and inhaling subterranean vapors, she would go into a trance, during which the spirit of the god entered her body and spoke through her throat. Priests standing nearby would transcribe her oracular utterances, and convey them to petitioners who had piously come to seek her advice.

Generation after generation of priestesses performed this sacred function, until finally in the late days of the Roman Empire the oracle foretold her own doom. In A.D. 390 the Christian emperor Theodosius ordered the pagan temple shut.

A Fateful Journey

Centuries before Theodosius, the pious had come to Delphi as pilgrims to submit their questions to the oracle. One of these pilgrims was a man named Oedipus, a prince from the royal house of Corinth. A drunkard had once mocked him and said Oedipus was not the king's true son. Others might have shrugged off such a remark, but not Oedipus. Instead, the issue of his identity festered in his brain like a wound that would not heal. Finally, when he confronted his royal parents, they reassured him that he was really their child. But self-doubt continued to consume him. Ultimately, he decided to journey to Delphi to ask an unimpeachable source.

But when he asked the priestess who his real parents were, she deflected his question and instead gave him an answer he hadn't counted on. "Should you go home," she said, "you will murder your father and marry your mother." Shocked and horrified at what he had heard, Oedipus stumbled out of the temple and, instead of heading back to Corinth, turned instead toward the city of Thebes, hoping thereby to avert the prophecy's fulfillment.

On the road he encountered an old man traveling in a carriage and accompanied by a guard. "Make way!" shouted the old man. "Make way, yourself!" retorted Oedipus angrily, still distraught over what the oracle had told him. But the old man did not make way, and in a fit of rage Oedipus struck him down and slew him and killed his entourage. Then, dusting himself off, Oedipus continued on his way.

The Riddle of the Sphinx

For weeks she had sat by the edge of the road guarding the way to Thebes. She was a monster—part serpent, part eagle, part lion—and the Greeks called her the Sphinx. To each traveler who came down the road she posed a riddle, posed it in her screeching voice, flapping her wings, whipping her serpentine tail, baring her leonine teeth. And each time she posed the riddle, the traveler failed, one after the other, and was slain.

And now young Oedipus came, fresh from Delphi, Apollo's home. He stood before the Sphinx.

"What creature is it," she hissed, "that at morning walks on four, at noon on two, and at evening on three?" There was silence then, and she seemed to savor it with her tongue as she readied to pounce.

But Oedipus smiled. He had always loved solving puzzles, even in the days when he was a small child growing up in the palace.

"What *is* it?" he mused, almost playfully, and then cunningly replied. "It is man," he said, "who as a baby goes on all fours, as an adult walks on two feet, and at the end of his days hobbles on three—his two weary legs and a cane!"

There was no need for the Sphinx to declare him right. She shrieked at his answer and straightway leaped to her death from the edge of a cliff.

Oedipus, for his part, continued on his way to Thebes, where he was welcomed by the populace as their savior for having slain the riddling beast. In gratitude they gave him the hand of their newly widowed queen, and made him their sovereign.

But as the years wore on, famine and pestilence crept over the kingdom like a slowly advancing shadow. In desperation, Oedipus appealed to the oracle of Delphi for guidance. The land is polluted, he was told, and will not be cleansed until the murderer of Thebes's former king is found and punished.

So, determined as ever to find the answer to things, Oedipus became a detective and investigated the crime, not relenting even when others, including his own wife, begged him to stop. In the end, he discovered how his infant origins had been obscured by abandonment and adoption. The man he had slain on the road to Thebes was, in fact, his very own father and Thebes's king. The widowed queen he later married was his birth mother. Thus the prophecy was fulfilled. Blinded by his own hand when he discovered the horrible truth, Oedipus would wander the earth in torment.

Oedipus had been quick to answer the Sphinx's riddle. Yet he did not know the answer was himself. At morning he was a baby abandoned, at noon a strutting man, at evening a humbled blind man leaning on a cane. It is easy to match a word neatly to its definition, harder to read the definition in our very own lives, to see the abstraction in flesh and bone, *our* flesh and bone.

Poor Oedipus, who knew "man" but not himself: the self quick to strike out and kill, the self quick to answer and proud of its alacrity, even as it hastens on its own destruction.

Poor Oedipus who, to make wrongs right, questioned others to find who murdered Thebes's former king only to learn that he himself was the very murderer he sought. Poor compulsive Oedipus, who would not rest until he found the answer that destroyed him, as only truth can sometimes destroy, the man who blinded himself when at last he saw.

Many who read Sophocles's play *Oedipus the King* superficially conclude that Oedipus was *fated* to suffer these things, that he was the victim of an inescapable destiny that imposed itself upon his life. But that is not the case. In forecasting events, the oracle of Apollo no more causes the future than a weatherman makes the weather. What the oracle did was *foresee* what would happen to us, given the character we possess and the circumstances we find ourselves in. It is from that humanistic inter-play of character and circumstance that our destiny comes. Thus, to quote Shakespeare, our destiny lies "not in the stars, but in ourselves." Had Oedipus known himself as readily as he knew the abstract defini-tion of man, he might have sidestepped tragedy. But he did not, and tragedy followed.

Each of us walks the road to Thebes. No, we will not kill an old king or marry a widowed queen after slaying a monster. But we will need to come to terms with who we are, because the ancient equation still applies: character + circumstance = destiny. Circumstances may not be of our choosing, but our character is ours to mold.

As Rich as Croesus

Centuries after Oedipus stopped at Delphi, some other visitors came for a stay. They had been sent on a mission by their king, the fabulously wealthy Croesus of Lydia, who ruled ancient Turkey. Croesus wanted to know if he should invade the territory of the Persians, his neighbors, and so sought the advice of the most revered oracle in Greece.

Before doing so, however, he had had a visitor of his own, an Athenian wise man named Solon. Solon had been touring the world, and had decided to make a stopover in Croesus's kingdom. Croesus was absolutely delighted to have such a distinguished visitor, and invited Solon to be his houseguest. The next morning he took Solon on a personal tour of his royal treasury. After showing off all his wealth, Croesus asked, "Whom would you regard as the most fortunate man in all the world?" Solon replied by naming an obscure Greek who had raised a fine family before dying in battle.

Somewhat put off, Croesus persisted and asked Solon who his second choice would be. Solon then replied by naming two more obscure

Greeks who had died and been honored after performing an act of filial piety. Thoroughly frustrated, Croesus (who had assumed he would have at least ranked second) insisted on an immediate explanation. Solon then patiently explained that we ought not to regard anyone as fortunate until we see him dead, for good fortune today can easily be followed by bad fortune tomorrow. Thus, by still being alive, Croesus could not qualify for a place on the all-time list of happiest men. And history proved Solon right.

When Croesus later queried the oracle of Delphi and asked if he should invade his neighbors, the oracle replied, "If you cross the river that separates your two kingdoms, a mighty empire will fall." Delighted with the news, Croesus raised an army and crossed the border dividing Lydia from Persia. Of course, the oracle was right. A mighty empire *did* fall, only it was Croesus's!

Like Oedipus, Croesus had acted on a false assumption. The oracle told Oedipus not to go back home. Oedipus assumed home was Corinth, not realizing that he was really born in Thebes. Croesus assumed that the empire that would fall would be his enemy's, not realizing that it might be his own. Both jumped to conclusions and paid heavily for their haste. Oedipus was exiled, and Croesus became a prisoner of war. Each had trusted in his strength, but failed to assess his weakness—the weakness of hasty judgment.

Of course, we shouldn't be too hard on Oedipus and Croesus. They were, after all, only human, making the kind of mistakes you or I might make if we were in their place. But that's the point. The making of such mistakes is part of the human condition. To be human is to be imperfect, flawed. Yet if we acknowledge that fact in all humility, we may yet be able to save ourselves from making the really big mistakes that could tragically alter our lives.

The Wisest Man in the World

Socrates had a favorite story he used to tell people when they asked how he became a philosopher. According to the story, a friend of his once went to Delphi and asked the oracle if there was anyone wiser than Socrates. The oracle simply replied no. When Socrates's friend told him this, Socrates was incredulous. "How could I possibly be the wisest man on Earth? I don't know anything," he said in amazement. And, to prove the oracle wrong, Socrates decided to question a few people until he found someone who knew more than he did. The problem was, when he interrogated people, he soon discovered they really knew very little. They might *think* they were wise, but after a little questioning it soon became obvious that their thinking was inconsistent and they really did not even understand the meaning of the words they used to expound their basic beliefs.

As a result of his survey, Socrates was forced to conclude that he was in fact the wisest man in the world, not because he knew so much, but because he knew that he knew so little. After all, we only have the right to consider ourselves wise when we acknowledge the depth of our ignorance, and then begin the search for truth, for only when we admit how little we know can we begin to grow in wisdom.

The Bible tells us "the fear of the Lord is the beginning of wisdom." To Socrates, the beginning of wisdom was the frank admission of our own ignorance—followed by the determination to do something about it.

The Allegory of the Cave

Socrates's student, Plato, tells us of a cave where men dwelt from childhood, shackled so they could see only an inner wall. For them the shadows that moved across that wall were the whole of reality.

Little did they know that all the shadows were created by the guards who held them prisoner. The prisoners did not know that behind them a fire burned and that the guards held up silhouettes before the flames that were projected on the walls as shadows.

Seeing the shadows every day of their lives, the prisoners grew familiar with them and learned their names. They prized their knowledge of shadows and called it wisdom. And they were rewarded by their guards for what they learned.

But then one day a prisoner broke free. With determination and strength, he crawled up the cave's sloping floor to its mouth. His eyes, accustomed only to darkness and dim flickers, were hurt by the sharp daylight that met them. But then he dared to go out, at first with his eyes averted to the ground to avoid the blinding daylight. He looked at natural shadows and then illuminated forms and then, finally, the sky above.

Soon he understood that what he had been learning all his life in the cave was a lie. He now knew the difference between shadow and truth, and held reality in his hands in the warming light of the sun.

As time passed, he yearned to share this new knowledge with his former friends, to free them too from the bondage of darkness, from the shadows they believed were true, from the masters who had deceived them. But to do this he had to reenter the cave.

He stumbled upon his reentry; his eyes were no longer accustomed to the darkness. But following the downward slope of the cave's floor, his eyes growing accustomed to the dark, he eventually found his way back to the place of his former imprisonment. There he struggled to release his friends from their chains, and passionately urged them to follow him to freedom.

But even as he tried to release them, they ridiculed him for rejecting what everyone knew with certainty was the truth. They even called him mad. And if he applied force to drag them toward the cave's mouth, they resisted with equal force. And when he persisted, some struck out and even tried to kill him.

All of us willingly dwell in such a cave. The fact is hard, almost impossible, to accept, because all our lives we have known no other reality. Our days have been spent learning illusions and our teachers have rewarded us well. Our existence has been made easier by the lies we have accepted.

Yet is it enough in life to be a content prisoner? And if we choose freedom instead, how shall we break our chains? And once free, how will we find the light? The goal for each of us will be different though the ascent will be the same: follow the upward path to the sun. Even in the darkest midnight, the sun awaits. It waits for us.

The Cave of the Cyclops

Caves were something the hero Ulysses knew about from personal experience. They weren't an allegory as they were for Plato, but a dangerous reality. Homer narrates the story in the ninth book, or chapter, of *The Odyssey*.

As the story goes, Ulysses was on his way home from Troy when he and his men chanced upon a seemingly deserted island. Venturing inland they found a cave stocked with cheese and equipped with pens for goats and sheep—the homestead of a shepherd. But when the shepherd came home with his flocks, Ulysses and his men were terrified—the shepherd was a hideous giant with a single eye growing out of the middle of his forehead. First, the giant rolled a huge boulder over the mouth of the cave to shut it. Then, after briefly asking who his uninvited guests were, the giant, known as the Cyclops, reached down, snatched up two of Ulysses's men as though they were puppies and dashed them into the ground. Afterward, he ate them.

"What's *your* name?" the giant then asked, turning to Ulysses. Thinking fast, for that was his forte, Ulysses replied, "Oh, *me*? My name is NoMan. And by the way, why don't you have some of this good Greek wine I've brought with me?"

"Thanks," said the giant, sloshing down the whole wineskin. Licking his lips, he added, "I'll return the favor by eating you last."

The potent wine took effect, and that's when Ulysses decided to make his move. As the drunken giant lay sprawled out on the floor, Ulysses found a wooden stake at the back of the cave. After sharpening the end, he held it in a fire until it glowed white-hot. With the stake poised vertically over the giant's single eye, Ulysses and his men plunged it in and spun it around.

The screams of the awakened Cyclops reverberated from the walls of the cave as he groped in his blindness to find his persecutors, who by now had hidden in the cave's recesses. Soon the screaming caught the attention of the other giants who lived on the island. Out of curiosity they followed the sound to its source and now stood outside the sealed entrance to the cave.

"Are you all right?' they called. "Is anyone hurting you?"

"NoMan is hurting me!" the Cyclops shouted back.

"Well, if no man is hurting you," they concluded, "you certainly don't need our help," and they went on their way.

Ulysses had blinded the Cyclops and evened the odds, but he and his men still needed to devise a method of escape. The mouth of the cave, after all, was still blocked by the immense boulder that only the mighty Cyclops could budge. Ulysses concentrated and again came up with a plan, and an ingenious one at that. Knowing that the Cyclops had to let his flock out to pasture in the morning, Ulysses told his men to hang under the sheep as they made their way out. The next morning as the giant let his flock out, he patted their backs as they exited, thinking Ulysses and his men might be riding on them, not suspecting that they were really suspended underneath.

When Ulysses and his comrades made it to shore, they boarded their ships and cast off. But Ulysses couldn't resist taunting his ex captor. And so he shouted out his true name and identity. "Tell *that* to anyone," he yelled, "who asks who blinded you."

This proved an almost fatal error. When the giant heard Ulysses's voice he homed in on it like sonar, and hurled huge stones in the direction from which the sound had come, stones that fortunately dropped into the sea, barely missing Ulysses's ships.

Some might claim that Ulysses's use of the name NoMan had simply been a clever trick. But it was not just a trick. When Ulysses was trapped in the cave's darkness, he was indeed NoMan. Only by escaping from darkness into light could he become Someone again. The cry he later uttered as he sailed victorious from the Cyclops's isle, the cry that proudly proclaimed his ancestry and homeland, "My name is Ulysses, son of Laertes, and I call the island of Ithaca my home!" was no mere boasting. No, because it proclaimed (though even he himself did not know it) his return into being. In his darkest hour, Ulysses had reached inside himself to find the means to his liberation, and from those inner resources of strength reclaimed his identity.

We are all conceived in darkness, but to be born we must struggle to the light. For each of us there are two births: our entry into the physical world and our entry into the world of the spirit. Our first birth grants us life without our even willing it. But our second birth must be deliberately sought.

Weakness vs. Strength

The search for self-knowledge requires that we identify our personal strengths and weaknesses. Only by so doing can we truly take measure of who we are, and who we can become. From an acknowledgment of our strengths can come the resolve to excel; from a recognition of our weaknesses can come the good sense to avoid extremes.

Alas, if it were only that simple! The ancient Greeks were perceptive enough to see that our strengths and weaknesses are often two sides of the same coin: a strength if carried to excess can become a weakness. If Oedipus, for example, had not been intellectually brilliant, he never would have solved the riddle of the Sphinx and gone on to become the incestuous husband of his own mother. And if he had not been a compassionate ruler, he never would have tried to save his newfound subjects from pestilence and plague by searching for the murderer who turned out to be himself. Intelligence and compassion—two worthy qualities that can become fatal flaws. Yet, the Greeks would be quick to add, how can we *not* want such qualities, and what would we be without them? Thus the paradox of man; our very virtues are the seeds of our vices. *Men* is but *de* in disguise. (How ironic that philologists refer to these little words as "particles"—from the weight of such tiny particles swing the balances of our lives.)

The Labors of Hercules

Like the hero Achilles, Hercules's parentage was mixed: his mother was a mortal named Alcmene; his father was none other than the great god Zeus. Like Achilles, he was a man without an existential country. He was stronger than an ordinary mortal because a god's blood flowed through his veins, but he was weaker than a god because he had to die someday. He was a citizen of neither land, an eternal wanderer across the psychic landscape. Perhaps it is for this reason that his personality so fascinated the ancient Greeks who identified themselves with him both because of his human qualities and their own divine aspirations.

Mythology tells us that, in a fit of madness, Hercules killed his wife and three children. (The madness had been induced by Zeus's wife, Hera, over the jealousy she harbored against Alcmene, Zeus's paramour.)

To atone for his sin, Hercules traveled to Delphi, where he was told that he must serve out his penance as the slave of a king. The king, whose name was Eurystheus, demanded that Hercules perform a series of impossible missions called the Twelve Labors.

The First Labor was to kill the savage Nemean Lion, whose skin was impervious to any weapon. The Second Labor was to slay a multiheaded serpentine swamp-beast called the Hydra, whose heads could grow back if they were cut off. The Third Labor was to catch the fleet Ceryneian Deer that had hooves of bronze and antlers of gold. The Fourth Labor was to capture the fierce Erymanthian Boar. The Fifth was to clean out the manure-filled Augean Stables. The Sixth was to kill the death-dealing Stymphalian Birds, whose feathers fell like knives from the sky. The Seventh was to tame the Cretan Bull. The Eighth was to seize the flesh-eating Horses of Diomedes. The Ninth was to steal the chastity belt of Hippolyta, queen of the man-hating Amazons. The Tenth was to rustle the Cattle of Geryon, a three-bodied monster. The Eleventh was to pick the Apples of the Hesperides, which grew on a magical tree at the edge of the world. And the Twelfth, last, and most dangerous Labor was to go to the kingdom of the dead and drag back Hades's multiheaded watchdog, Cerberus, from Hades's gates.

Hercules accomplished all of these Labors. He wrestled the Nemean Lion to the death, cauterized the severed heads of the Hydra to prevent them from regrowing, shot the Ceryneian Deer with a swift arrow, chased down the Erymanthian Boar, flushed out the Augean Stables by diverting a river, shocked the Stymphalian Birds with a sonic explosion, rode the Cretan Bull like a bronco, corralled the Horses of Diomedes, charmed Hippolyta out of her belt, stampeded the Cattle of Geryon, persuaded Atlas to pick the Hesperides' apples (while Hercules held the heavens up), and captured Cerberus by feeding the hound dog-food laced with tranquilizers.

No wonder the Greeks admired Hercules, not only for his strength, stamina, and ingenuity, but also for his determination to go on and complete each and every task, as impossible as they all seemed. His was the story of humanity, facing one obstacle after another but never quitting. It was that determination that was his greatest strength, just as such determination can be ours as we grapple with the labors of our own lives, labors that some days seem as difficult to us as Hercules's must have seemed to him. Maybe there's no Nemean Lion for us to wrestle, but everyday heroism comes in smaller but no less heroic sizes.

Heroes in Stone

Hercules is also one of the most enduring figures in Greek art. His exploits are illustrated on Greek vases just as his physique is displayed in Greek sculpture. His larger-than-life-size image reminds us of the potential strength we all possess, a strength we could actualize if only we tapped it. To know ourselves is not only to know the self we are, but also the self we can become.

Our power to surmount obstacles was conveyed by an unknown Greek artist in his bronze portrait of a boxer. Unlike the coolly objective *Discus Thrower* whose body is unscathed, the *Bronze Boxer* embodies a brutalizing sport, especially as it was fought in the Hellenistic Age—with lead-lined gloves. The boxer slumps wearily, his shoulders hunched, his head twisted sideways as though responding sluggishly to a roar from the crowd. Bleeding, his face bears the insignia of his profession: cauliflower ears, a broken nose, and scars. He is an aging veteran, struggling on despite pain and disfigurement, answering the call to fight one more time, because that is what life demands.

The Discus Thrower belongs to a time that believed all too confidently in the certainty of victory, the *Bronze Boxer* to a later but wiser generation that had paid dearly for its wisdom. The *Bronze Boxer* and other statues of the post-classical period reveal that Greek artists in no way abandoned the humanistic quest, the search to discover what it means to be human. In defiantly affirming the quest for self-knowledge, they continued to expand the definition of the human spirit. Like the battered boxer, we too must continue to fight. The search for self-discovery will never be an easy quest.

Seeking Self-Knowledge

Travelers to Delphi came to Apollo's oracle bearing questions. Most wanted to know what the future held. Had they only paid more attention to the words printed above the temple door, "Know thyself," they would have gotten their answer free of charge. To know ourselves is the best way to know our future. It is our relative strengths and our relative weaknesses that most accurately predict our destiny. Therefore, the most valuable direction to turn our questions is inward. Fate is not something necessarily imposed on us from outside, but more truly emanates from within.

By gaining self-knowledge we gain the ability to know when to press hard (the pursuit of excellence) and when to pull back (the practice of moderation). Self-knowledge informs us of our limits. The racecar driver, the test pilot, the deep-sea diver, and the astronaut all must acknowledge their limits if they are to survive. It is no less true for us as we navigate the landscape of everyday life. Just as it is important to know what self-knowledge is in the Greek sense, it is critical to know what it is not.

It is not a kind of psychotherapy that explores our personal past history for episodes that have damaged our psyches. The ancient Greeks clearly anticipated modern psychotherapy. Early in *The Iliad*, Achilles's goddess-mother, Thetis, comes ashore to Troy to ask him what is troubling him, even though she already knows. She realizes he can find peace only by unburdening himself to her in words. But that is not what the search for self-knowledge is really all about. It is not about looking for the sharp-edged shards of the past. Self-knowledge implies the search for more general characteristics of personality that are predictive of future behavior and future choices. Had Achilles understood what drove him in life, for example, his life might not have ended in tragedy.

No, the search for self-knowledge does not involve psychotherapy. Nor is it shallow self-help, the all-too-common approach to the daily problems we face today. The search for self-knowledge is simultaneously deeper and broader since it does not just address situations in the present but surveys the full range of possible interactions between the kind of people we are and the types of situations we may encounter. It does not hand us a superficial bandage to cover our wounds, but asks us how and why we hurt ourselves in the first place. It asks us to courageously probe our human strengths and weaknesses and to find within ourselves the means of our cure, freely admitting our own ignorance even as we seek illumination.

CHAPTER 5

THE FIFTH PILLAR
RATIONALISM

The fifth pillar of Greek wisdom is rationalism. Rationalism means the use of reason. Unlike rationalization, which uses reason to explain away behavior, rationalism employs uncompromising logic to discover the truth. To the ancient Greeks, rationalism was the primary means of gaining self-knowledge. Rather than waiting for enlightenment to come from divine revelation, the Greeks turned to an illuminating instrument closer at hand, the power of human intelligence.

The Birth of Athens

Ages before the city of Athens was called by that name, two gods competed for the allegiance of its citizens. The first god was Poseidon, the god of the sea, who made a spring of water gush up from the summit of the Acropolis. The water signified mastery over the sea, which Poseidon said he would grant the people in exchange for their worship. The other deity was Athena, the goddess of wisdom. The gift she promised was the olive tree, which she made miraculously sprout from the Acropolis's rocky soil.

The people chose Athena, and named their city Athens for her. In a later day, Athena's victory over Poseidon would be celebrated in sculpture on the western pediment of the Parthenon, Athena's greatest temple.

But why had the people chosen the lowly olive over maritime power? The answer is the olive was not lowly at all. They recognized it as a major source of nutrition, even as it continues to be in the Mediterranean world today, whether eaten whole or crushed to make oil. In ancient Greece the oil was used not only for eating and cooking, but also as a cleansing agent and emollient for the skin. Greek athletes, for example, would rub their bodies with olive oil after a workout and then scrape the dirt and sweat from their skin. Some have even seen in the olive tree a symbol for the Greek personality: hardy and tough, because it can take root and thrive even in meager soil, and individualistic, because no two olive tree trunks look exactly the same.

But the greatest virtue of the olive, and the reason why Athena made it her gift, was its value as a source of fuel. Indeed, apart from wood, it was the most common fuel of the ancient Mediterranean. It was olive oil that filled and lit the lamps of Greece. And therein lay its connection with Athena. The burning oil of the olive produced light that banished the darkness, just as intelligence can banish the darkness of ignorance.

To honor Athena, the Athenians erected temples in her name and placed her portrait on their silver coins. Her helmet (she defended her city in times of war) was decorated on each coin with silver olive leaves. And on the back, a sprig of olive filled one corner, just above the shoulder of the wise old owl, who was Athena's pet.

Athens, however, honored Athena most by becoming, especially in the fifth century B.C., a city of light illuminated by intellectual energy, the home of Greece's Golden Age.

Yet who was this goddess Athena? One myth made her the daughter of Zeus, the king of the gods, and Metis, a goddess whose name meant "insight." According to the story, Zeus impregnated Metis, but—fearing the offspring she might have—swallowed her. Afterwards, he developed a splitting headache, so bad that his head had to literally be split by an axe to relieve the pressure! Out of Zeus's cranium emerged the figure of Athena, fully armed for battle. Her origin, then, was truly cerebral.

The wisdom Athena stood for, however, was not wisdom in the ancient Near Eastern or Biblical sense: the revered distillation of ancient tradition. Instead, it was the capacity to apply the power of critical intelligence to solve problems. Indeed, it might be more accurate to speak of Athena as the goddess of intelligence rather than wisdom. She was a problem-solving goddess, representing a distinctively human faculty. Her favorites included Ulysses, the hero whose nimble mind outwitted the Cyclops and whose craftiness contrived the wooden horse that caused Troy's fall. According to one myth, she so loved man that she breathed life into him when he was first created by Prometheus out of water and clay.

To honor her in *our* lives, we must, to put it bluntly, use the brains God gave us. To carry us through the darkness we must light Athena's lamp, until it leads us to the sun.

Penelope's Web

Penelope, Ulysses's wife, was as wily as her husband. In the long years after the Trojan War, she never lost hope that someday her warrior husband would return. The nobles of his kingdom, however, were eager to take his place, and had camped out in his palace, all the while pressing Penelope to choose one of them to be her new husband and the future king of Ithaca.

To hold them at bay, Penelope said she could not contemplate marriage until she had first woven a shroud for her aged father-in-law. The suitors respectfully acceded to her request, assuming the task wouldn't take long. But for three whole years she sat at her loom weaving. Finally, in the fourth year, one of her maids gave her secret away: what Penelope wove during the day she unraveled at night. The suitors then confronted her, but she had already bought three years of time, enough to permit her shipwrecked husband to start on his homeward journey.

When Ulysses finally reached Ithaca, he knew he would have to confront the hostile suitors in battle since they all wished him dead. His problem was that he was outnumbered. In Ulysses's corner: Ulysses himself, his young son, and a loyal swineherd or two. In his opponents' corner: 118 well-armed nobles. The solution (and it was Athena's idea) was for him to return home disguised as an old, homeless beggar, exactly the kind of person no one would suspect of being the former king. The disguise would allow Ulysses to sort out those who were still faithful to him from those who were not, including even Penelope. After all, twenty years had passed since a much younger Ulysses had sailed for Troy. In the interval, Ulysses wondered, had his wife acted more like chaste Artemis or sensuous Aphrodite? He would watch and see.

Once he discovered Penelope *had* been a faithful wife, Ulysses tricked and trapped the suitors and slew them. In turn, Penelope had her own doubts about whether this man who now claimed to be her long-lost husband was just a fortune-hunter or the Ulysses she had once married. So she decided to use some trickery of her own to find out.

"Welcome home, dear," she said. "I'll have the maid bring our bed out here into the patio so we can sleep beneath the stars."

"Hold on a minute!" Ulysses said. "What do you mean, 'bring out the bed'? I carved the bedpost with my own hands from the trunk of an olive tree that was rooted to the ground. It was a symbol of our marriage bond that was meant to be everlasting. How *dare* you cut the bed from the tree!"

That was all Penelope needed to hear. The secret of the bed was a secret that no one else shared. This stranger was her beloved Ulysses. And with that declaration, the two embraced and went to bed to express the love they had been so long denied. To make their love more complete, Athena even held back the dawn so their night together would be longer. Both had survived the long years by drawing upon their innate intelligence and, by so doing, had triumphed over adversity.

The Dark Labyrinth

Another ancient story of love and reason took place on Crete, the largest of the Greek isles.

Crete's most feared king was Minos. Minos's troubles began when his wife, Pasiphaë, fell in love with someone else. But it was no ordinary human being she craved. Instead, it was a mighty bull. Desiring to entice the bull to satisfy her lust, Pasiphaë turned for help to Daedalus, the master craftsman of the palace. Though he feared the consequences of her unnatural passion, Daedalus obediently complied and invented the means by which she might fulfill her longing. With timber and hide he constructed a replica of a cow and, placing it in a meadow, told Pasiphaë to position herself inside. The two indeed mated—woman and bull— just as Pasiphaë had desired, and from the mating the queen became pregnant and gave birth. The progeny she bore, however, was no ordinary child. It had the body of a baby boy and the head of a bull calf.

When King Minos saw it he was horrified, but could not bear to slay the creature fearing that it might represent some omen of the gods. He let it live, but he ordered it hidden from the light of day so that no one else might see it. Summoning Daedalus, he commanded him to design a special prison from which no one could ever escape. However, the prison must have neither locks nor bars.

Daedalus accomplished this by designing an ingenious maze. So intricate was the pattern of its passageways, that once a man entered it he could never again trace his way back out, being drawn instead inexorably toward its center.

The maze was called the Labyrinth; the man-bull (in time he grew to full stature) was called the Minotaur, named for King Minos and the Greek word for bull.

Minos had other children, human children, and among them a fine son. When the son was grown to manhood, he was sent on a mission to the Greek mainland, to the city of Athens. But while he was there he was killed. The Athenians said his death was an accident; others said that the killing was a deliberate assassination.

Minos believed the worst and determined to exact vengeance upon the Athenians, and his power was great enough for him to do exactly that, because he was the master of a maritime empire.

By his decree, every year seven young men and seven young women—the finest flowers of Athenian youth—had to be sent on a ship to the royal Cretan city of Knossos. There they would be led through the entrance to the Labyrinth. Slowly the windings of the maze would draw them in toward its center where the Minotaur, and death, waited.

For many years this deadly ritual was reenacted. But one year a prince of Athens named Theseus resolved to end the executions. He begged his father to let him go as one of the chosen youths. Theseus believed he was brave and strong enough to kill the monster and thus free his people from their death sentence. Theseus's father finally relented and let his son go.

It was the custom in Crete, before the Athenian hostages were led into the maze, to present them to Minos, who explained to them the heinous crime for which their lives would serve as expiation.

On the day Theseus was brought to the throne room, it so happened that Minos's lovely daughter, Ariadne, was there. When her eyes beheld

Theseus's godlike form, she instantly fell in love with him. But she also knew he would surely die once he was led into the Labyrinth.

Remembering that Daedalus had designed the Labyrinth, Ariadne went to him to appeal for mercy and advice on how she might save the life of the young man she loved. Daedalus felt compassion for the young princess. But he feared what would happen should King Minos learn he had given aid to a hostage.

"Ariadne," Daedalus told her, "if the young man you love is hero enough he will be able to slay the monster. Destiny will have its way. But if he does succeed, let me give you the means by which he may save his life. For even with the monster dead, he will be doomed to die as the Labyrinth's prisoner. Take a spool of thread and secretly slip it to the young man you love. Whisper to him to tie it to the Labyrinth's door as he enters, and then let it out bit by bit as he walks through the darkness. If he kills the monster, he can then follow the path of the thread back to its beginning...and freedom."

Ariadne did as she had been told, giving the spool of thread to her young prince and passing on Daedalus's instructions.

Theseus lived up to her hopes. Once inside the Labyrinth, he did as she had advised, tying the thread to the door and letting it slowly unwind as he moved down the corridors to where the Minotaur waited.

They met in the darkness. Neither Theseus nor the monster knew what the other was like except that he was his enemy and was strong and must be slain. Theseus grabbed what seemed to be the horns of the beast and twisted them, with all his muscles straining, to snap the monster's neck. And all the while the Minotaur fought back, struggling to gouge his human foe. The Labyrinth echoed with the bellowing and hard breathing of the struggle. And then, with a snap and a final groan, it was over, and the monster lay dead.

On his hands and knees, Theseus found the spool on the floor and, standing upright, followed with his fingers as the thread led him and his companions back through the dark corridors. When he reached the entrance, Ariadne was there where she had waited, praying for his safe return.

Leading his Athenian comrades with him and taking Ariadne by the hand, Theseus found his ship and set sail for Athens. When news of the escape and the Minotaur's death reached Minos, the king was enraged and screamed out that Daedalus be brought to him, believing that only the man who had designed the maze could have given away its secret to others. Daedalus and his son Icarus were arrested. Only later did Minos discover that his daughter too was gone. But it was too late. The ship was already carrying Ariadne and her lover away.

Now that the Minotaur is dead, the Labyrinth is empty, and the ship that bore Theseus and Ariadne across the sea is gone, are there no more mazes to solve, or monsters to slay, no more triumphs over darkness to celebrate?

Observe the ingenuity of Daedalus's original design. The way into the Labyrinth is easy; all can find the path. It is the coming out once we have entered that is hard. It is in the nature of a maze to lead us to its center, like life itself that draws us—if we let it—ever inward. And finally, when the maze of life has worked its will upon us, we meet the monster.

Who then is this creature—half human, half beast? Who is it, then, if not ourselves? In that deadly encounter we must summon up all our strength, all the power of our being, as whole-man grapples with half-man, to see who will triumph.

To be sure, we can refuse the battle, and condemn ourselves to wander forever through passageways leading nowhere. Yet if life is forgiving, it will bring us to the heart of the Labyrinth and give us the chance to be brave.

To escape, however, courage alone will not be enough, nor confidence, nor daring. Once our enemy is defeated, we will still need to find our way out of the maze. We will need reason to help us, a thread from Ariadne, bestowed upon us long before we knew what it meant, tied to the door we entered before we understood its value. It is reason that can finally lead us out of the dark Labyrinth into the light.

An excess of rationalism, however, can prove fatal. Too much intellectualism, for example, almost took the life of Daedalus. After Daedalus gave away the secret of the Labyrinth and fled from Crete, King Minos pursued him, tracking him all the way to Sicily. Knowing Daedalus was in hiding, Minos offered a prize to the man who could weave a thread through the inner spirals of a conch shell. King Cocalus of Sicily, who granted Daedalus asylum, offered to solve the puzzle and showed the shell to Daedalus. Unable to resist the intellectual challenge, Daedalus then drilled a hole in one end of the conch shell and inserted an ant to which he had glued a slender thread. When the ant exited the other end of the shell, Cocalus turned the shell over to Minos and demanded his reward. Realizing that only Daedalus, the designer of the Labyrinth, could have solved this intricate puzzle, Minos demanded Cocalus surrender his guest.

"Of course," agreed Cocalus, "but why don't you first take a nice hot bath before dinner?" Minos foolishly agreed, not suspecting that Cocalus's daughters would scald him to death with boiling water. Luckily, Daedalus escaped with his life. Too much rationalism can be dangerous, but its opposite—too much emotion—can also be destructive.

The Battle of the Lapiths and Centaurs

In far-off Thessaly there lived a tribe called the Lapiths, and their king was Pirithoüs. Theseus, the future slayer of the Minotaur, was his friend.

When Pirithoüs decided to marry, he invited the neighboring tribes to the wedding festival. Among the invited guests were the Centaurs, a strange race that was part human and part animal, human down to the hips, but with hips joined to the body of a horse.

When the Centaurs arrived at the wedding, they drank of the abundant wine and became intoxicated. Freed from their inhibitions and loosened from all moral restraint, they acted on impulse, seizing and galloping off with the beautiful bride and bridesmaids, much to the consternation of Pirithoüs and the other Lapith men, who rose to defend their women. Theseus, who was there, joined in the fray.

The battle between the Lapiths and the Centaurs was fierce. The struggle would later be depicted in a sculpture on the temple of Zeus at Olympia, and on the Parthenon in Athens.

In the end, the Lapiths triumphed and drove off their enemies.

Some have interpreted the portrayal of the Lapiths and Centaurs in art as political propaganda. According to their theory, the Lapiths represent the Greeks themselves; the Centaurs represent the Persians, whom they had recently defeated in war. Ideologically, the Lapiths stood for Greek civilization and its defenders, who sought to preserve law and order; the Centaurs stood for the Persian forces of barbarism, which were bent on destruction.

But we can discover even more by contemplating the nature of the Centaurs, who, like the Minotaur, were only half human and driven by bestial and brutish impulse, violent and unrestrained emotion. The Lapiths, on the other hand, were fully human and governed by rationality. The battle was thus symbolic of a fundamental conflict within human nature: the conflict between emotion and reason, between impulse and logic.

Thessaly, the land where the battle took place, is not so far-off after all. The war between the Lapiths and Centaurs still rages in each of us. The battleground is the self. To what extent should we let our emotions rule our lives? To what extent should we let our lives be governed by reason?

Such questions, of course, are inherently flawed because they presume we can deliberately make a choice, that we can neatly dispense a role to each. The ancient Greeks might have said we can, or, better, that we must try.

For most of their history, the Greeks were not such fools as to think we are masters of our lives. Many tragic heroes and heroines prove the opposite, and the Greeks were attentive to their tragedies. The protagonists offer proof not just that our emotions can get the better of us, but that they can dominate, even destroy, our lives. Beware of excess, Apollo warned, in the full realization that, as human beings, we are prone to that very thing.

Our danger lies in presuming that we are pure Lapith, that we can fabricate our lives entirely out of cool reason and, by so doing, guarantee their perfection. Our nature, however, comes closer to that of the Centaur. Man, half this, half that, is a hot-blooded creature endowed with a brain. Which part of us will triumph in the end will determine our fate and the fate of civilization itself.

Mad as Hell

Emotional heat is evident in the lives of three characters from Greek myth—Achilles, Antigone, and Medea—and the irrational fire that consumed them.

Achilles

Achilles is the central character in Homer's *The Iliad*. Besides being the earliest surviving work of European literature, *The Iliad* is also the West's first psychological novel. Achilles may be its central character, but the driving force and true subject of the epic is an emotion, as the author makes clear. "Sing, Goddess, of the wrath of Achilles, and its deadly consequences," he cries. It is the consequences of this emotion that the poet pursues, how one man's anger "hurled the souls of brave heroes into hell, and left their corpses as carrion for vultures and dogs."

All because of an argument. Achilles had spent nine years fighting at Troy and risking his life for glory. But each time the spoils of war were divided up, it was not Achilles, but his haughty commander-in-chief, Agamemnon, who got more.

During a raiding party on an outlying village, women were taken to serve as concubines for the invading army. Agamemnon got his pick of the women, and that's when the trouble began. A devastating epidemic broke out in the Greek camp, sent by Apollo, because the woman Agamemnon picked to be his concubine was the daughter of a priest. To save the army from dying, Agamemnon was compelled to give his concubine back to her father, but not before he found a substitute. Since all the women had already been distributed, Agamemnon decided to choose his substitute by taking Achilles's woman. Insulted, Achilles declared he would sail for home. After absorbing nine years of abuse, his pride could take no more.

With Achilles out of action, Greek casualties began to mount. Agamemnon offered to make amends, but Achilles turned a deaf ear. Finally Achilles's best friend and comrade, Patroclus, offered to step in and take Achilles's place. Obsessed with his own hurt pride and relentless in his anger, Achilles thoughtlessly allowed Patroclus to go into battle in his stead, and Patroclus was killed. No amount of grieving or revenge proved enough to fill the hole left in Achilles's heart by Patroclus's death.

Antigone

Antigone was Oedipus's daughter, and inherited her father's obstinacy and passion. During her father's exile, Antigone's two brothers fought with each other for control of Thebes. In a final battle, they died at each other's hand. The new king, Antigone's uncle Creon, decreed that one brother, who defended Thebes, should be given a state funeral; the other, who had attacked the city, should be left unburied, his corpse to rot on the battlefield and his soul to wander forever without rest. Furthermore, Creon decreed, should anyone bury the man, that person would be executed.

To spite Creon, Antigone decided to defy his order, choosing to obey God's law rather than man's. She covered her brother's body with earth, flaunting Creon's heartless edict.

New to the throne and intolerant of any challenge to his authority, Creon then ordered Antigone to be entombed alive. Creon's son, who was engaged to Antigone, rushed to free her, only to find that she had taken her own life by hanging herself in a final act of defiance. The heartbroken young man then killed himself with his sword. Upon hearing the news of her son's death, Creon's wife became the next to take her life. At the end of Sophocles's dramatic version of the story, Creon sits on the throne, alone and desolate, the victim of his own willfulness.

Medea

Medea was a sorceress. As the playwright Euripides tells the tale, she fell in love with an adventurer named Jason, who came to her father's kingdom in search of the Golden Fleece. Medea helped him secure the Fleece, and when both of them were pursued at sea by her father, she killed her own brother and threw the parts of his mutilated body into the water so her father would be compelled to stop and gather them, thus allowing her and her lover to escape.

However, now that Jason had the Fleece, he no longer needed Medea and grew weary of her company. To advance his own career, he married the princess of a different kingdom where he had been given welcome.

Medea, spurned, now contrived her revenge. She sent a wedding gift to Jason's bride, a robe smeared with a corrosive poison that ate away her skin and killed her. Then to punish Jason all the more, she took their two children and butchered them. At the conclusion of Euripides's tragedy, the sorceress Medea flies into the sky on a chariot drawn by dragons.

A Deadly Trio

Achilles, Antigone, Medea—a trio of mythic characters who illustrate the cost of fiery emotion. They reveal in larger-than-life terms what can happen when a life is taken over by raw passion. Though we may never rise to their heroic heights, or sink to their hateful depths, their biographies warn us to control our emotions with reason before we hurt ourselves or those we love.

Paradise Lost

The Athenians of the Golden Age believed that reason must prevail over unbridled emotion if civilization itself is to survive and prosper. Reason must guide emotion with its logical principles in the same way a rider controls a horse with his reins.

They graphically depicted this idea in art in a 524-foot sculpted belt of marble that ran around the tops of the walls of Athena's sanctuary. The frieze shows a parade that was held in Athena's honor every four years. As selected young men of Athens proudly ride their mounts, we see a striking contrast between the emotional detachment of their faces and the fiery expressions on the heads of the horses. Throughout, rational order prevails, in tribute to the guiding spirit of Athena.

The faces of the men and their bodies are also obedient to a logical principle that flourished in their times, a principle that viewed beauty as mathematically expressible. It is for this reason that all their faces are the same, because all beauty was answerable to the same formula of perfection. The sculptor Polycleitus even wrote a book, now lost, giving the proportions of the perfect human body.

The Golden Age was an age of idealism, and idealism was a function of reason. The Golden Age was also an era of intense creativity produced by harnessing the energy of the mind. Never before in history and never since has so much of lasting intellectual value been created by so few. The fact is that most of what we call classical Greek literature and art was made in one city, Athens, that at its peak had a population of only about forty thousand citizens. Yet among these were giants: the dramatists Aeschylus, Sophocles, and Euripides in tragedy, and Aristophanes in comedy; the philosophers Socrates and young Plato; the historians Herodotus (on temporary stay) and Thucydides; the sculptors Myron, Polycleitus, and Phidias, sculptor of the Parthenon; and Ictinus and Callicrates, architectural designers of the temple itself.

Why all this happened in the span of one century is hard to say. The only analogy that comes to mind is Florence in the days of the Renaissance. Wealth and leisure were two of the decisive factors, and patriotic pride another. A rich pool of talent—a fortuitous genetic accident—a fourth. But surely one of the most important factors was the set of principles by which the Athenians lived, especially humanism (already described), individualism (yet to be discussed), and rationalism (the subject of this chapter). Not coincidentally, these same principles, combined with those same factors, inspired the Italian Renaissance, which witnessed the rebirth of the classical ideal. When Michelangelo sought to represent Adam on the ceiling of the Sistine Chapel, he may have deliberately taken as his model a reclining male nude from the Parthenon—pausing only to reverse the figure's pose from right to left to signal that his was a Christian rather than a pagan age.

Presiding over Athens in the middle of the fifth century B.C. was its leading statesman, Pericles, who cared about his city's culture in the same way that Florence's Lorenzo de Medici cared about his. It was Athens's *il magnifico*, Pericles, who directed the urban renewal project atop the Acropolis that saw shining new temples take the place of those destroyed by the invading Persians at the century's beginning. But Pericles, like Lorenzo, was also an architect of politics. It was Pericles who transformed what had been a voluntary association of free Greek cities into an empire arbitrarily ruled by Athens. Ultimately, it was this imperialistic policy that provoked a war with Sparta that left Athens militarily and psychologically defeated at the century's end.

Pericles and his fellow Athenians should have foreseen that defeat. The real-life scenario they acted out was the very same one they had watched time and time again as spectators in Athens's great theater. It was the standard narrative formula of Greek tragedy: a character who enjoys wealth (*olbos*) exhibits arrogance (*hubris*); that arrogance in turn inspires an act of blind folly (*ate*) that invites the vengeance (*nemesis*) of the gods, gods who stand ever-ready to teach man he has gone too far. What the Athenians failed to recognize is that such a lesson can apply to a state as well as to an individual. Intoxicated by affluence, Athens acted arrogantly toward its neighbors, committing one act of extremism after another, acts that finally incited a deadly war that lasted for more than twenty-five years, the so-called Peloponnesian War between Athens and Sparta.

How could Athens, a city of reason, have been so blind?

The answer is that the Athenians were simply human beings, not gods, a distinction they tragically forgot on the road to success. They had surrounded themselves with an artificial environment of perfect, even godlike, images, until they began to believe that they were as perfect and godlike as the figures they had fashioned out of stone. But they were not faultless marble; they were fallible flesh, more Centaur than Lapith, and not exempt from heaven's law.

Even the Parthenon was a deception, for there is not a single straight line in it. Instead, it is an optical illusion in which every surface is deliberately distorted to compensate for flaws in human vision. Had the superstructure, for example, been made perfectly horizontal, it would have looked sagging and weak; therefore, it was curved slightly upwards in order to appear straight and true. The Parthenon's architects were not building a temple on the Acropolis at all; they were building a temple in the human mind and were willing to distort reality to placate the senses. Man was, the sophist Protagoras said, the measure of all things. But all things could be a beautiful lie.

The virtual reality of the classical age was a dangerous exercise in self-delusion in which the Athenians convinced themselves that they were an invincible master race that deserved to rule other men. So can our dreams deceive us and blind us to the truth, destroying us in the end. It was a lesson a young man named Phaëthon learned to his grief.

The Myth of Phaëthon

Helios was the god of the sun who drove the sun's fiery chariot across the sky. Helios had also fathered a child from a sea nymph, Clymene. When their child, Phaëthon, grew to manhood, his mother made the mistake of telling him who his father really was.

Doubting her word, Phaëthon determined to discover for himself his father's true identity. He would journey eastward toward the horizon until he came to Helios's palace. There he would demand to know the truth.

When he saw Phaëthon, Helios freely admitted being his father and, to prove it, offered to grant Phaëthon any wish. Alas, Phaëthon said his wish was to drive the chariot of the sun across the sky. His father tried desperately to dissuade him: driving the fiery team of horses that drew the sun was not a task for beginners, and certainly not for a teenager. But Phaëthon insisted, and the fateful promise had been uttered and could not be taken back, so the youth mounted the chariot and took the reins in his hands.

As soon as he did, the horses burst out of the gate and soared into the sky. Phaëthon tried his best to restrain and keep them on their appointed course, but the team sensed that hands other than Helios's held the reins, timid and fearful hands that were not their master's. Careening, the chariot of the sun suddenly dipped low, so low it scorched the earth.

Zeus, looking down from Mt. Olympus, saw to his horror what was happening; the earth would soon be incinerated. He had to act quickly, and had no other choice. So he aimed his thunderbolt and blasted Phaëthon from the chariot. The boy was buried, they say, where he struck the ground, and on his tombstone were put these words:

> Here lies Phaëthon, driver of his father's chariot.
> Though he could not steer it, still he dared great things.

Sunrise on the Acropolis

Each morning the rising sun illuminates the eastern face of the Parthenon, just as it has for twenty-five centuries.

The sculptor Phidias designed the eastern pediment of the Parthenon to tell the story of Athena's birth from Zeus's brain. As Athena is born, a messenger rushes to deliver the news to the gods. In a corner far to the right, the chariot of the setting moon dips over the western horizon, its team of horses weary and breathing hard; in a corner to the left, the chariot of the sun begins to make its ascent. It is sunrise, the time of Athena's birth, a glorious sunrise for Athens, a sunrise for all Greece.

It was a shining moment not only for Greece but for humanity, but it was a moment that was lost because man aimed too high. Reason is only a tool, and it is so easily manipulated by blind ambition.

With the reins of reason in our hands, we—like Phaëthon and the Athenians—dare to drive the chariot of the sun. Hitched to our national chariot are the headstrong steeds of science and technology champing at the bit, urging us to exploit nature and perfect it as we see fit. "The sky's the limit," they seem to say. The gate before us opens, and Zeus watches from on high.

The Greeks and the Irrational

Despite their passionate commitment to the use of reason, the ancient Greeks also acknowledged the vital role of the irrational. Indeed, their very passion to know the truth was itself irrational. Stripped of emotion, Greek civilization would be far less interesting; in fact, it is doubtful it would have thrived. Emotion is one thing, the search for truth, we might think, another. But that is not how the Greeks saw it.

The Eleusinian Mysteries

The Eleusinian Mysteries were one of the best-kept secrets of antiquity. The Mysteries, or mystic rites, derive their name from the holy site where they took place, a place on the outskirts of Athens called Eleusis. Tradition tells that the earth-goddess Demeter came to Eleusis while searching for her daughter Persephone, whom Hades had kidnapped. Disguised as a poor old woman, Demeter was shown hospitality by the locals and in gratitude revealed her true identity. A temple was then built there in her honor. When she finally found her daughter, Persephone taught the citizens of Eleusis the arts of agriculture. They were the first people to whom she conveyed these secrets.

For centuries thereafter, Demeter and Persephone were worshiped at Eleusis in an annual ceremony celebrating the fertility of the earth and the miraculous generation of vegetative life. In a special sanctuary known as the Telesterion, worshippers were initiated into the cult, and vowed never to reveal the substance of its secret rites. Our word "mystery," in fact, comes from the Greek word *múein*, which meant "to keep one's lips sealed." So binding was the vow and so overwhelming the mystic experience that accompanied it that we know next to nothing of what actually happened in the dark confines of the sanctuary. Some scholars believe worshippers were shown a single, radiant sheaf of wheat and received luminous intimations of a joy that awaited them in the afterlife, even as Demeter had herself triumphed over the god of death, even as from a seemingly dead husk the greening life of a seed springs forth. Such intimations were not given by rational means but by an experience so profound that words could not describe it.

Even the philosopher Plato, who argued that a knowledge of what he called "the Good" could only come from an advanced exercise of reason, held that the Good itself was, like the splendor of the sun, an ineffable presence that transcended reason. To view its rising, however, the philosopher had to ascend on the feet of logic.

The God of Ecstasy

If transcendence marked the worship of Demeter, ecstasy distinguished the worship of Dionysus. The word ecstasy comes from Greek, and literally means "to stand outside oneself." Ecstasy was associated with the cult of Dionysus because Dionysus was the god who, as giver of wine, freed human beings of their inhibitions. He was thus an irrational god who liberated humanity from the confines of convention. His female devotees, called Maenads, even went into frenzies in which they ate the raw flesh of animals that they killed and tore apart with their hands.

In his book *Beyond Good and Evil,* the nineteenth-century German philosopher Friedrich Nietzsche identified Dionysus as the polar opposite of the coolly intellectual god Apollo. For a civilization (including modern civilization) to be vital, both an Apollonian and a Dionysian principle must coexist, but of the two, Nietzsche argued, the Dionysian must prevail if creative civic life is to burgeon like a vine of ripe grapes bursting with juice.

In festivals associated with the growing of grapes for wine, the Greeks honored Dionysus, who went on to become the patron god of dramas inspired by the liberated mind. But there were also conservative tendencies in Greek culture that viewed the entry of Dionysus into Greek religion as a threat to the behavior of the masses.

Euripides's tragedy *The Bacchae* describes how a king named Pentheus tried early on to stop the growth of Dionysus's cult in the belief that it was a subversive force. In the final act, Pentheus is slain by Dionysus's Maenads, who in their frenzy tear the king limb from limb. Despite this gory episode, Dionysus continued to be revered because the Greeks identified him with a dark but potent energy trapped within their souls, an energy that rightly defied the suffocating restraints of excessive reason.

Dionysus remains a god today, and a dangerous one at that. He is the god of illicit drugs and of alcohol, the god of mobs and unthinkable ideas. We must somehow come to terms with him, because in his mirror we see our own faces. It may not be a face we want to know, but it is ours nonetheless. If we refuse to recognize him, he will still exist and punish us, like Pentheus, for our obstinacy and our denial. Somehow we must find a strategy for living with him while not renouncing Apollo. Reason alone would be bloodless and cold, but without reason we would only be beasts.

Exercising Reason

In exploring the self, the seeker of knowledge uses the torch of reason to penetrate to the lowest and darkest level of his emotions. The ancient Greeks clearly saw that we are not totally rational creatures, but are in fact driven by emotional needs and appetites. They were the first in world history to view life as a battleground between reason and emotion. Yet if we are captives of our emotions, we are not in full control over our lives. How, then, can we gain such control?

The honest answer is, we may not be able to gain *full* control. The Athenians of the fifth century B.C. labored under that illusion to their historic regret. But to acknowledge that such emotions exist, and may need to be checked, is to gain at least *partial* control. Not that the ancient Greeks would ever have wanted to be totally free of emotion, since to be emotionally sterilized would have been to be purged of joy as well as sorrow. But at the same time, they realized that emotions are volatile and can cause us more pain than we might otherwise want.

How, then, are we to apply the principle of rationalism to our everyday lives?

First, by recognizing exactly what the ancient Greeks did. Our lives are a tug-of-war between feelings and logic. Merely acting on our emotions does not guarantee us happiness. And logic alone does not make us human.

We must employ the power of reason to solve those problems that are amenable to reason while acknowledging that reason has its limits and cannot solve all problems. Many problems cannot be addressed in the human brain; they can only be handled by the human heart.

We must keep Athena's tool, reason, at the ready in our mental tool-box, and not let it rust. It is the instrument of first choice in dealing with an issue. Athena's true gift, after all, wasn't "doing it the way it's always been done." Ulysses knew that when, as NoMan, he tricked the Cyclops and escaped from the cave. Intelligence can mean finding a new way, solving an old problem with a solution never before tried, or even imagined. Intelligence and rationalism can thus be doors to freedom.

CHAPTER 6

THE SIXTH PILLAR
RESTLESS CURIOSITY

Restless curiosity, the sixth pillar of Greek wisdom, is the compulsive desire to know the truth. The capacity to be rational is worthless, the Greeks believed, unless we use it to generate courageous questions about ourselves and our world.

Ajax's Prayer

On the blood-stained plain before the city of Troy, a fierce battle raged between the warriors of Greece and their Trojan enemies. To give the Trojans a temporary advantage, Zeus decided to blind the Greek army by cloaking the battlefield in darkness. In the midst of that darkness, a rough and ready Greek warrior named Ajax cried out, directing a prayer to heaven:

> Father Zeus, deliver us from the darkness and make
> the sky clear. Let us see with our eyes. Slay us
> in the light, if slay us you must!

Ajax is so tormented by the darkness that he prays for light, even if the coming of that light will bring about his death. This compulsive need to see, first expressed in Homer's *The Iliad*, was characteristic of the ancient Greek nation. Ironically, tradition relates that Homer was himself blind, but that did not stop his inner eye from seeing into the nature of man. To fulfill our humanity, the poet tells us, we must wrestle with reality, even at the cost of death. To dare less is to be less.

The Death of Laocoön

As the Trojan War dragged into its tenth year with the two sides evenly matched, the Greek army decided to win by deception. On Ulysses's advice, they constructed a huge wooden horse and loaded its spacious interior with commandos. The idea was to trick the Trojans into taking the horse into the city. Once inside the walls, the commandos would wait for nightfall, open a trap door, and stealthily clamber down a rope ladder. Then they would find and light torches, and signal to their ships lying offshore. The Trojans would be caught off guard, and the city could be looted and burned.

Following their plan, the Greek army packed up and set sail, leaving the wooden horse on the deserted beach. When the Trojans looked out from their battlements the next morning, they thought the Greeks had finally given up and gone home. As a crowd of Trojans milled about the horse in wonderment, others hauled over a Greek deserter they had found in hiding. No deserter, he was in fact planted there by the Greeks to trick the Trojans into taking the bait.

"The horse is a gift to the gods," the spy said. "If you bring it into your city, you'll never have to fear the Greeks again." Of course, to get the horse into Troy, the Trojans had to dismantle their gates, leaving the city defenseless—exactly the thing the Greeks wanted. But the Trojans were too drunk with victory to worry over such details. "Let's bring it in!" they shouted.

Just then a Trojan priest named Laocoön stepped up and silenced the eager crowd. "Beware of Greeks even when they are bearing gifts," he warned. Laocoön was suspicious of the wooden horse and what it might portend. "There's something unnatural here," he thought, "something we need to investigate." And, taking aim, he hurled a spear and struck the horse, making its hollow body shudder and the commandos inside gasp. "I thought I heard something," he said.

But before he could do more, the gods who hated Troy and wanted it to fall sent two serpents up from the sea. Unnoticed, they slithered their way across the beach to where Laocoön and his sons stood. Then, coiling their immense bodies around the three, they crushed them to death.

Laocoön had dared to pose a vital question, and paid dearly for his inquiring mind.

The Trojans, taking the priest's death as a sign from heaven, and ignoring any dangers the horse might pose, brought it, and doom, into the city.

The Song of the Sirens

After the fall of Troy, the victorious Greeks loaded their ships with treasure and sailed for home. Helen, the seductive cause of the war, was put onboard her husband's ship, destined for a life of domesticity and contrition for her wayward affair.

Eventually, all the Greek warriors returned home, all except Ulysses, who would endure a decade of maritime travail before reaching Ithaca and reclaiming his wife. On his homeward voyage, Ulysses had to overcome many obstacles and resist many temptations. Notable among those temptations was his encounter with the Sirens.

The Sirens were female creatures who bewitched passing mariners with their melodious singing. They sat in a flowering meadow surrounded by the rotting corpses of those who had been lured to their shores by their song.

Ulysses's course would take him by the Sirens's coast, but a friendly goddess had told him how to escape death. "Plug the ears of your crewmen with wax so they won't be able to hear," she had said. "Then they won't be tempted to go there. As for you," she added, "if you wish to hear the Sirens's song, have your men tie you to the mast, and tell them that, if you order them to release you, they should tie you all the tighter."

Of course, Ulysses could have plugged *his* ears with wax too, and never heard the Sirens's song. But he wanted to have the experience and live to tell about it. Ulysses was a man who wanted to soak up new experiences. Homer tells us that at the beginning of *The Odyssey*, when he introduces his protagonist to us as a man who "saw the cities of many men and learned their minds." Unlike impetuous Achilles, Ulysses was a thinking-man's hero who craved the adventure of exploring the unknown.

The nineteenth-century English poet Alfred, Lord Tennyson captured his spirit in a poem titled with the hero's name. Tennyson imagined Ulysses back home on Ithaca, safe and secure...and bored. A senior citizen, he longs for one final adventure. And so he gathers a crew of graying age-mates to set sail once more. Here are Ulysses's parting words from that poem:

> Death closes all: but something ere the end,
> Some work of noble note, may yet be done,
> Not unbecoming men that strove with gods.
> The light begins to twinkle from the rocks:
> The long day wanes: the slow moon climbs: the deep
> Moans round with many voices. Come, my friends,
> 'Tis not too late to seek a newer world.
> Push off, and sitting well in order smite

The sounding furrows; for my purpose holds
To sail beyond the sunset, and the baths
Of all the western stars, until I die.
It may be that the gulfs will wash us down:
It may be we shall touch the Happy Isles,
And see the great Achilles, whom we knew.
Tho' much is taken, much abides; and tho'
We are not now that strength which in old days
Moved earth and heaven; that which we are, we are;
One equal temper of heroic hearts,
Made weak by time and fate, but strong in will
To strive, to seek, to find, and not to yield.

"To strive, to seek, to find, and not to yield"—such a Ulysses could never have passed up hearing the Sirens's song.

But what was their special attraction? Was it simply the extraordinary beauty of their singing? Apparently not. At least in Ulysses's case, the Sirens custom-designed their song to catch their prey. Intellectual curiosity, they knew, was Ulysses's "Achilles heel" (to mix epic metaphors), so they appealed to his curious mind. "We know all that happened on the plains of Troy," they sang, "and all that will happen on Earth." It was thus the past and the future that they dangled before him to lure him to their shore.

The pull of the past and future was irresistible, and Ulysses strained at his bonds, shouting for his men to release him. But, as instructed, they tied him tighter still, 'til the sound of the Sirens's voices blended into the sound of the foaming sea.

Had Ulysses gone to them, he would have died, for the past and future, Homer infers, can kill. They rob us of the present, the only dimension in which we can truly live. Dwell nostalgically on a past that we can no longer inhabit, daydream about a future that has not come to pass, and the present slips through our fingers, forever lost. They tantalize us—past and future—precisely because we are human and curious. But precisely because we are human we must resist becoming their slaves.

The Education of Telemachus

Even as Ulysses was making his way home over the sea, his young son Telemachus had left home and was searching for word of his father. Telemachus did not know if Ulysses was alive or dead. He had been just a baby when his father had gone to war, a war that had lasted ten years. And for another decade, long after all the other warriors had been accounted for, Ulysses's whereabouts remained unknown. Telemachus had never had a father to model his life on, to learn what it meant to be a warrior and a man. And now the situation in Ithaca was going from bad to worse, as the arrogant nobles who had taken over his father's palace pressed his mother to choose one of them as her new husband. At a loss to know what to do, Telemachus was visited by Athena, the goddess of the intellect, who urged him to search for his father's whereabouts, to find out whether he was alive or dead. Athena inspired young Telemachus with an active curiosity, the impulse to find concrete answers to the questions that haunted his life. Curiosity, you see, by itself is impotent until it is wedded to action. Otherwise, we are paralyzed by worry and inertia.

The mission Athena sends Telemachus on is a bit of a paradox, however. As the goddess of knowledge, Athena already knows where Ulysses is, that he's started on his homeward way. Why not tell Telemachus? Why make him search for the answer himself?

The reason is that the answers to the really important questions in life can only have meaning for us if we search for them by ourselves. A psychotherapist might readily describe to us our problem after a single visit, but curing that problem requires that we discover the answer for ourselves. In reality, the quest *is* the healing. The destination itself may be merely incidental.

By leaving the comfort of home, by risking a dangerous sea voyage, by trekking to the palaces of mighty nobles and acting like the prince he was, Telemachus grew up and became his father's son. Travel, they say, is the best education. For Telemachus, the search for answers became the road to maturity.

Psyche's Mistake

If curiosity can help us grow, sometimes it can be our undoing. According to this story, Psyche was about to be sacrificed to a monster when a mysterious god saved her, a god she was not permitted to see. He transported her to his palace where each night he made love to her, but always in total darkness so Psyche could not view his body or face.

Eventually, Psyche's curiosity got the better of her. "Who is this creature," she asked herself, "who saved my life and now so passionately loves me?" One night while her lover slept, Psyche crept from their bed and found an oil lamp. Lighting it, she brought it close to the bed so she could see her savior's face. In the flickering light of the flame she saw he was more handsome and perfect than she could have dreamed.

But as she held the lamp in her hand, a drop of hot oil spilled out and fell upon his cheek, waking him. Seeing Psyche standing over him in the light, and realizing that his identity was now known to her, he rose and vanished into the night, leaving her weeping and alone. In Greek, the name Psyche means "soul," and in the story Psyche's lover is named Eros, or "passion." The myth thus tells of the soul's quest for passion, for love.

Eros flees from Psyche when the soul demands too much: to see its face in the light, to know its name, to trap its unseen essence within the bounds of definition. The object of our love can be experienced but never owned. If we seek to possess it, it will instantly vanish from our bed.

The Undiscover'd Country

The story of Psyche is not only a love story, but it is also a tale of intellectual obsession. Others were possessed by that same obsession, but for reasons that were not erotic.

As the circle of the known expands, the surface tangent to it, the unknown, expands as well. Thus, the more we know, the more we realize we have yet to learn. The ancient Greeks, who were impelled by a restless curiosity, discovered much, but each new discovery inspired them to seek more. They were a race of explorers, probing the outer world of the physical universe and the inner world of the human spirit. At each new discovery another new frontier beckoned, the "undiscover'd country" to which they owed their natural allegiance.

The decades between 750 and 600 B.C. witnessed an era of maritime exploration as Greek adventurers planted colonies on the Mediterranean's far-flung shores. Beginning in the late 600s, a new breed of thinkers called philosophers, literally "lovers of wisdom" (from *phílos*, "lover," and *sophía*, "wisdom"), began to speculate on the nature of the universe. "What is the world made of?" they asked. "And what is its most essential ingredient?"

For some, the answer was water; for others, air; for still others, fire. And for others, all of these in combination with earth. Some spoke in numbers, others of infinity, and still others of an invisible mind at work. By the mid-fifth century, the atomic theory was born.

What all these philosophers had in common was their curiosity, a hunger to know that had little to do with anything practical, but everything to do with all things real. Theirs was an abstract quest across a cosmic sea in a ship called reason.

The Search for Truth

By the mid-fifth century, Greek philosophers turned from theorizing about the nature of the universe to theorizing about the nature of man. Some philosophers called Sophists proposed that what we call reality is merely a construct designed by men and a projection of their particular values. Accordingly, morality is not absolute, but relative to place and time. What is legal in Sparta, for example, may be unlawful in Athens. Therefore, he who is wise will learn the prevailing mores of the place he is in and use this knowledge to his advantage, molding public opinion through the art of persuasion to gain personal and material success.

Others, like Socrates the stonecutter, scorned riches and argued that truth is an absolute that cannot be altered by mere opinion. It is our moral duty, Socrates believed, to search for that shining and universal truth, for without it our lives will lack meaning and direction. Truth is not malleable and gray like clay, but hard and white like marble. We must quarry that marble and then define its contours as sharply as we can. Socrates's hammer and chisel were question and answer, deftly wielded and persistently applied until the truth emerged, or its opposite—falsity—was revealed. Rational discourse was impossible, he believed, until we have accurately defined our terms. Socrates, moreover, believed this quest for truth must be social; the truth cannot be found by the individual in isolation, but only through the democratic give-and-take of spirited dialogue and debate.

During his long career, many found Socrates's methods offensive, especially when he embarrassed them by showing how little they really knew about the very things, including politics, they regarded themselves as expert in. This was particularly true in the tense years of the war between Athens and Sparta, and in the dark days that followed, when many would have preferred not to be reminded of their shortcomings.

Eventually, Socrates's enemies brought him to trial. The charge: corrupting young people and not believing in the gods of the state. "Corrupting young people" because many young Athenian men admired his courage in taking on the establishment, and "not believing in the gods of the state" because Socrates, though pious, obeyed the dictates of his own conscience most of all.

The prejudiced jury found Socrates guilty. Then the plaintiffs and the defendant had to propose alternative penalties for the jury's consideration. Socrates's enemies took the radical step of proposing the death penalty, thinking to force Socrates into proposing a serious penalty on his own, though not as severe a one. But Socrates surprised them. Sticking to his principles, he proposed that he actually be rewarded for what he viewed as a public service, but then backed off a little by agreeing to pay only a modest fine, the money to be supplied by his friends.

As for speaking out no more, as many would have wanted, Socrates refused. His reason was, "An unexamined life isn't a life fit for a man to live." To be human, after all, means asking questions; to be silent is to be less than human.

The jury of 501 men condemned him to death by a vote of more than two to one. Imprisoned and awaiting execution, Socrates refused his friends' offer to help him escape because he felt he ought to abide by the laws of the city that had nurtured him. Eventually, the poisonous juice of the hemlock was administered and he died.

Socrates's last words were preserved by his student Plato. Transcribed by Plato, his address to the jury is often called *The Apology*, but it is no apology. Instead, it is a defiant defense of the principles by which he lived. (*Apologia* is simply the Greek word for a defense speech.)

Paradoxically, Socrates's life was extinguished by the city of light that created him. But times had changed, and Athenian idealism had been corrupted by money and power, and then by defeat.

Though Socrates died, his values lived on not only in his words, but in the example of his courageous life and death. Even today he reminds us that a life that cannot be questioned isn't worth living, and that to live such a life is to sell out our humanity.

The Hellenistic Age

Socrates died in 399 B.C., five years after the end of the war between Athens and Sparta. During the rest of the century, Greece drifted without a moral compass. Idealism had died with Athens, and there was no new city or philosophy to fill the vacuum. By 338 B.C., the once-free cities of Greece were conquered by Philip of Macedon and made into his kingdom. With Philip's assassination in 336 B.C., his twenty-year-old son Alexander took his place, and went on to lead Greece in a holy war against the Persian Empire, which fell to his army. Alexander's kingdom then stretched eastward to India and southward to Egypt, and Greece became but one small part of a brave new world in which West and East, Europe and Asia, were joined. This world, the Hellenistic, was geographically fragmented by Alexander's death in 323 B.C., but remained culturally unified by the politics he had initiated in his lifetime, including the building of Greek-style cities as beacons of Hellenism across the breadth of his empire.

Despite the wrenching political changes of the fourth century B.C., Greek culture remained undefeated, and philosophy found a new voice. If Athenian idealism had failed, a new set of principles had to be found to guide people's lives. In searching for answers, Hellenistic philosophers turned from intellectual abstractions to sensual reality. New philosophies arose based upon the senses, upon pleasure and pain. Stoicism taught that we must transcend life's pain; Epicureanism taught that we must seek out life's most lasting pleasures.

If the perfection of classical art was a lie, then art must be more true to life, portraying its fleshly agony and carnal ecstasy, in poses as extreme and shocking as reality itself. The golden mask of the classical age was torn from the face of the human race by new sculptors who ached for the truth and dared proclaim it.

Laocoön Reborn

One of the most striking statues of the Hellenistic Age shows Laocoön and his two sons. Laocoön and his boys are attacked by twin serpents that have wrapped their thick bodies around the helpless three. The trio struggles in vain, crying out for help that will never come. We too stand impotent as we helplessly watch their struggle.

There is no symmetry here, the statue tells us, because there is no symmetry on Earth, nor justice or mercy. Why, we must ask, was this story told in stone one thousand years after Troy fell? Because the myth still made sense to the later Greeks. It spoke to their times about a world that is not perfect, where decency and innocence are betrayed, where the good suffer and the evil prosper, where serpents creep silently up from the sea. It is a world where our most important questions go unanswered, but where, if we are to remain human, we must continue to ask until we die.

Being Curious

Exercising reason does not mean simply solving old problems; it also means finding problems that haven't yet been identified. That's where curiosity comes in. Curiosity means asking the unasked question; it means pinpointing the anomaly that no one else has seen. But it also means acting courageously by being willing to speak your mind. There are questions people don't want asked, anomalies they don't want noticed. And when those people are powerful, being curious ceases to be an academic exercise, and becomes an exercise in courage.

Socrates knew that when he burst the anti-intellectual bubble of Athens's pretentious elite. He also paid the price. In today's world, scientists and inventors are paid for their curiosity. In fact, all good scientists and inventors have to be restlessly curious, and determined, if they're going to be good. But a creative society needs the curious in every walk of life because, as things change, new approaches are needed to make them better. Twenty-six centuries ago, the philosopher Heraclitus spoke of constant change when he said, "You can't step twice into the same stream." Today, however, the social stream is flowing even faster, demanding more new answers and more new questions.

Our children start out curious, but educational regimentation soon cures them of that. Yet if they become sullenly rebellious or dully compliant, where will the questioners of tomorrow come from? Those of us who are parents and teachers have a duty to keep childlike curiosity and wonderment alive both in our offspring and in ourselves. And as citizens and consumers, we need to keep questioning too, always demanding to know why the reality is so far removed from the ideal.

CHAPTER 7

THE SEVENTH PILLAR
THE LOVE OF FREEDOM

The seventh pillar of Greek wisdom is the love of freedom.

To the ancient Greeks, freedom was as necessary for life as the air we breathe.

Asking vital questions is possible only if we are free, for only in freedom can humanism thrive.

Wrestling with Proteus

Freedom, however, is not automatic. It must be fought for, as the following tale makes clear.

One of the earliest Greek visitors to Egypt was Menelaus, the king of Sparta and husband to Helen. After the Trojan War was over and the armies of Greece were heading home, Menelaus landed in Egypt. Homer does not say whether he went there by accident or design, but he does report that Menelaus had trouble leaving Egypt, becalmed on the island of Pharos just north of the delta of the Nile. Imagine the powerlessness the king must have felt—a conqueror of Troy defeated by a wind that never came.

Of course, pious warrior that he was, he concluded he must have offended some god or another and, having tried to propitiate as many gods as he could think of, he became more and more disconsolate when the wind remained unmoved.

It was then that Eidothea decided to save him. She was a sea nymph and the daughter of the Old Man of the Sea, Proteus. Why she took pity on Menelaus, Homer does not say, but he does provide the advice she gave. She told Menelaus to wait in ambush for her father and force him to reveal how Menelaus might escape.

Making Proteus talk, however, would be no easy matter, his daughter warned. Proteus could change into different creatures or even water or blazing fire. Menelaus was not put off by this seemingly impossible task, though. He was a hero and king, and had little other choice if he wished to get back home. So he and two trusty comrades hid and waited for Proteus to come ashore. And when he did, Menelaus captured him.

Sure enough, Proteus began to change: first into a fierce lion, then into a twisting serpent, then into a sleek leopard, and last into a wild boar. But still Menelaus held him fast. Then Proteus turned into running water to slip through the hero's grasp, but even that did not help. Finally he became a stout tree, but Menelaus locked his arms around the trunk and refused to let go.

In the end, just as Eidothea had foretold, Proteus returned to his original form, exhausted from having transformed himself into so many shapes. At that point Menelaus interrogated him. In response, Proteus revealed that Menelaus was being held prisoner on the island for having earlier failed to make offerings of gratitude to Egypt's gods. He must therefore sail back to the mainland and make the sacrifices that were due. And so he did, and thus gained freedom.

Only through struggle did Menelaus find the secret by which his freedom was won. It was not enough to make sacrifices on the island where he was marooned. He had, instead, to return to the place where he had gone wrong, to the shores he had turned his back on and forgotten. Only by returning to his beginnings could he lay claim to his future, and sail on to meet it.

To discover that truth, he had to hold on to old Proteus, maintaining his grip even when reality seemed to change before his very eyes. Then, and only then, could he be free.

Each of us must come to terms with our beginnings and wrestle with the present, however much it may change, in order that the future may be ours.

The Persian Wars

Besides Menelaus, there were other Greek heroes whose fight for freedom became legendary.

In 490 B.C. the freedom of Greece itself was threatened by a foreign invader, the Persians, or ancient Iranians, then the masters of the largest empire the world had ever seen. Hungry for more territory, the Persian king launched a naval attack on the Greek coast not far from Athens.

Rather than cowering behind their city's walls, the Athenians marched with their allies to the landing site. Under the command of a general named Miltiades, they charged the Persian camp, the first time Greeks had ever challenged the Persians in battle. Before this time, the mere mention of the name "Persian" had been enough to strike fear in soldiers' hearts.

One hundred and ninety-two Athenians died in that encounter, but sixty-four hundred Persians fell, and Greece won the battle and the war. The Greeks had triumphed because they were defending their homeland against a mercenary army. They also triumphed because they were defending their way of life. Defeat would have meant being enslaved to a tyrannical king; victory meant remaining free.

Ten years later, however, the Persians attacked again, this time with an amphibious force consisting of as many as three million men. On land, the Greeks were determined to hold a key pass at a place called Thermopylae. The pass was to be guarded by an advance party of perhaps seven thousand Greeks under the command of the Spartan king Leonidas. The Spartans were to wait for reinforcements. But before the reinforcements could arrive, a Greek traitor showed the Persians how to enter the pass from the rear and trap the Greeks inside. Seeing that the situation was hopeless, Leonidas ordered most of the men to withdraw, while he himself with three hundred veteran Spartan warriors defended the pass against overwhelming odds. They fought and died.

After the war was over and the Greeks had finally defeated the Persian aggressors, a gravestone was erected at Thermopylae to mark the spot where the Spartans fell. A simple epitaph read:

> Stranger, when you get to Sparta tell them
> we are still holding our position,
> obedient to their last command.

Not all the Greeks, however, had fought for freedom. Many, believing that the Persians would be the inevitable victor, had collaborated with the enemy. Among them were the people of the city of Caryae. At the war's end, in reprisal, the city of Caryae was besieged and captured, its men executed, and its women and children enslaved. Decades later a temple, the Erechtheum, was built atop the Acropolis of Athens. In place of six columns to support the roof, six statues were carved out of marble to symbolize the traitorous women of Caryae. The Caryatids, as they were called, were forced to carry the weight of the temple's superstructure on their heads in perpetual punishment for the treason they had committed. So heavy, the Greeks believed, must the punishment be for those too cowardly to risk their lives in defense of freedom.

Such a lesson bears repeating in any age, especially when the long passage of time distances people from the historic sacrifices that have made possible the way of life they enjoy.

The Flowering of Democracy

The way of life the Athenians enjoyed after the war was the way of democracy. Democracy was a Greek invention, and it flourished most of all in Athens, thanks to constitutional reforms enacted during the century before the Persian Wars.

As freedom is to the individual, so democracy is to the state. But the Athenians were wise enough to recognize that freedom and democracy, if they are to truly serve humanity, must be governed by self-discipline and self-restraint. Freedom, after all, is simply a condition; it does not dictate what we do with the freedom we possess. To be free can mean to be selfish, or to sacrifice on the behalf of others. The choice is ours. Like waxwinged Icarus we can skim the waves or chase the sun, and die either way, or we can choose the middle path. To be free is to be responsible for the lives we choose.

As for the individual, so for the state. A lynching is, after all, the purest form of democracy in action—majority rule. But it is repugnant to us because, democratic though it may be, it flies in the face of principles—the respect of life and an individual's sanctity and the honoring of due process and the rule of law—that we hold equally sacred.

Indeed, as Plato argued from the bitter experience of seeing his teacher Socrates killed, democracy is perhaps the most dangerous of political systems because it entrusts the making of decisions to a majority that can so easily be swayed by sordid emotion.

As we have already seen, the Athenians were human and therefore fallible. In the midst of their imperialistic quest and the war with Sparta that Athens had provoked, they built another temple on the Acropolis, this one dedicated to Athena Nike Apteros. Nike means "victory" (it survives today in the brand name for athletic gear). Apteros means "wingless." Because the goddess of Victory was normally represented *with* wings, the Athenians deliberately built a temple to her *without* wings, not wanting Victory to ever fly away and leave them. So it was the Temple of Athena, the *Wingless* Goddess of Victory.

The temple sat on the western abutment of the Acropolis, perched at its edge like a marble bird cage. But the goddess of victory did not stay inside for long. She left when the Athenians themselves became buoyant with victory over Persia.

The Greeks learned to their regret that we are most vulnerable not when we are weak but when we are strong. When we are strong, we are likely to commit acts of hubris, overreaching ourselves and bringing on destruction. Democracy, especially a materially successful democracy, thus contains within itself the seeds of its own destruction. But it is human to aspire, to reach for greatness. That is our special ironic talent, and if we did not exercise it we would cease to be human.

Another image of Victory, this time with wings, endures as one of the most dynamically dramatic works of Greek sculpture's history: the eight-foot-tall winged Victory of Samothrace, erected to commemorate a naval victory by Greece over Syria around 190 B.C., now in Paris at the Louvre. Victory is shown alighting on the prow of a ship. She faces out to sea, her chest thrust out, the wind blowing back her swirling gown and sweeping back her marble wings. Only her head is missing, but the rest remains, defying the ravages of time, standing in the face of an age-old wind, witnessing that final victory is indeed possible. Despite our accumulated failings, we must continue to struggle, continue to fly, continue to aspire to succeed.

Escape from Death

For the ancient Greeks who loved life so passionately, the greatest victory would have been the victory over death, to be free of its uncompromising power. The Greek love of freedom thus extended beyond the grave.

Ultimately the ancients had to acknowledge death's greater power. But their unfulfilled longing for eternal life manifested itself in different ways: through the creation of literature and art as instruments by which their spirit might endure, and through the performance of courageous deeds that would preserve their names in the memory of their countrymen. The defiance of death also inspired mythic tales in which gods or heroes sought valiantly to liberate those they loved from death's grip.

The Freeing of Persephone

At the edge of the world beside the great river that circles the earth there is a land beyond sunrise and sunset, a land where no time exists except forever. To this flat land, covered in thin, gray mist, all souls must travel; here lies the entrance to the underground realm of the dead.

Long ago, after Zeus defeated the Titans, he and his brothers divided up the world they would rule. Zeus chose the sky, and Poseidon chose the surging sea. Each would share the company of living creatures, mortal and immortal. But Hades, cheated by his partners, received only the land of the dead. His was a kingdom where nothing changed or grew, a kingdom of shapes without substance. Hands could reach out but never feel; arms could close but not embrace. Hades's honor was to rule in dark loneliness for all eternity.

At times, when he ached with loneliness, Hades would mount his black chariot, driving his four black stallions through the twisting chasms that led up to Earth's surface. Emerging, he would close his eyes and drink in the sun's radiance through his face, then dare to open his eyes to drink in with his mind Earth's forbidden beauty, its golden wheat fields and flowering meadows. In those days Earth lived in endless summer. Yet, in the end, Hades was always compelled to return to his own dark realm.

Once on such a journey, as his chariot raced across the sunlit land-scape, he saw a solitary young woman standing in a meadow. Her long hair was golden like the wheat, flowing in waves in the soft wind. Hades longed to take this figure in his arms, to join his loneliness to hers, to feel alive again as once he had so long ago before he had become monarch of the dead.

Again and again Hades returned to the same place, hoping to see her once more. Each time he did, it became harder for him to turn his steeds back, to return to his empty kingdom. Finally, seeing her again, his long-ing grew so much he could no longer contain himself. He whipped his team and hurled his chariot across the meadow. Sweeping her up into his strong arms, he plunged deep into a chasm and vanished from Earth.

But the creature Hades had abducted was no simple mortal. She was the daughter of Demeter, mistress of Earth's fertility. When Demeter dis-covered that her daughter was gone, she looked for her. Not finding her by day, Mother Demeter searched even into the night by torchlight, but to no avail. It seemed her daughter Persephone had disappeared from the face of the earth. Demeter thought only a god could have caused this to happen.

Determined to get her daughter back, she decided to use the one divine power that belonged to her, the power of fertility. She would with-hold her gift from the earth until her daughter was returned.

Until this time Earth had rejoiced in eternal summer, but now for the first time green things began to wither and the chill winds of autumn swept across the land. The human race that had never known need began to hunger from famine, and then to die. Even the gods themselves began to tremble, fearing there would be no more sacrifices for their altars, or even any mortals left to make offerings in their name.

Finally Zeus realized he must act to restore the order of things. Knowing his brother's secret, he ordered Hades to return Demeter's daughter. But Hades did not want to give her up and knew there was a way, despite Zeus, that he could keep her forever. Each day of her imprisonment, Hades offered Persephone food, knowing that once a soul partakes of food in the land of the dead that soul joins the company of the dead forever. Day after day Persephone refused, but finally she relented. From that day she was never to be free of Hades's power.

When Zeus learned what Hades had done he was enraged, especially because he still needed to placate the goddess of fertility. In the end, he arranged a compromise. Persephone would stay with Hades, but for only half the year. During the rest of each year she would live with her mother.

It is this compromise that explains the seasons. When Persephone returns to her mother, life returns to Earth. Spring is born, and then summer. But when Persephone leaves her mother to return to Hades, autumn and winter come.

At first, Persephone looked at her time in Hades's underground kingdom as imprisonment, and she longed to return to the bright surface of the earth. Yet each time she prepared to leave, Persephone saw Hades weep, and each time she returned to his kingdom, she saw joy on his face. Soon she realized that she was not abandoning summer when she left the earth's surface. For, rather than leaving summer behind, her coming to Hades's kingdom brought with it summer's radiant warmth. By returning to that dark world she became what she could never have been in the world above. To Hades, Persephone was all things, even life itself.

For his part, Hades came to know Persephone anew. At first she had been his possession. But over time through her tears, he came to know

Persephone for herself, and to love her. Less and less did Demeter's welcome make Persephone forget the man she had left behind. Each time Persephone took leave of Hades, she did so with greater regret and, even during her seasons in the sunlight, longed all the more to return.

So it was that the power of Aphrodite worked a miracle in the darkness, a miracle the queen of passion herself had not foreseen. She had made love come into being in the very presence of death.

The Rescue of Eurydice

Hades brought the lovely Persephone from the land of the living to the land of the dead to become his bride, but there was once another who sought to retrieve his bride from Hades's kingdom and return her to life. His name was Orpheus.

Orpheus was a musician, the like of which had never been heard on Earth before or since. His music, played in a woodland, could make distant trees rise up on their roots and walk so that their leaves might better hear. Even stones would move, crawling slowly across the ground, drawn forward by the beauty of his playing on the strings of the lyre. Orpheus was used to enchantment, playing the enchanter and seeing others bend to his will. But soon his skill in moving and persuading others would be tested as never before.

It was no wonder that beautiful Eurydice had been in love with him for months, had fallen captive to his music and longed to spend her life by his side listening as he played. All women envied her for knowing Orpheus the musician, the creator of the world's most exquisite sounds.

Not only did he compose songs for her, but their very lives together seemed to have become a composition he was writing, with harmonies built by their intertwined feelings. Orpheus and Eurydice, Eurydice and Orpheus, which one was the melody and which the harmony?

Orpheus himself played at their wedding as he and Eurydice met beneath the open sky and all gathered about to hear their spoken vows. Even the creatures of Nature chose to watch.

But as Eurydice approached Orpheus along the river bank and walked through the tall grasses, a serpent—quiet, unseen, subtle as the music Orpheus played—bit her ankle.

At first that bite seemed so innocent, a gentle sting, but soon the venom coursed silently through Eurydice's veins and she grew weak, collapsing finally into Orpheus's arms. Orpheus dropped his lyre, making the strings twang with a never-before-heard dissonance. Then all was silent.

It is said he mourned for her, sitting beside her still body, kneeling, sometimes raising up his lyre to play once again the songs that had moved her heart, songs that once had even moved the trees and cold stones, but nothing, no melody, could cause her to stir. In the face of death Orpheus's music had no power.

He sat there long after her family had carried her body away and buried it. He played the same song, touching the strings of the harp, the strings that had always yielded before, singing the words, long after any audience was left. Soon even the boughs of the trees seemed to withdraw, the stones to slowly pull away, until only Orpheus himself was there to hear his singing.

When morning came, the lyre lay there in the tall grass, the breeze blowing over its strings and stirring them to soft resonance. It seemed the grasses bent gently as though listening to the strings' soft hum.

It was in that last night that he first conceived the long, terrible journey to the land of the dead, the journey that is impossible for us to make while we are alive, but so easy when each of us has ceased living since our souls already know the way.

They say that, holding a new lyre, he performed on the way, ever seeking the west and the place of the setting sun and the entrance to Hades's domain.

Those who heard him said he had not changed, that he had actually put Eurydice's name out of his mind. (After all, they had only known each other a short time. They had never shared their lives as husband and wife will. Their life together had only been promises made but never fulfilled and, since one of those who had made the vows was already dead, they were promises that could be gladly forgotten, slipping away into the currents of Lethe, the river of forgetfulness.)

Only when audiences asked him to play the song that Eurydice had loved best, the song that he had composed for her, did Orpheus seem to hesitate and then, when finally he began to play, made all weep, even those who had never before heard her name.

It was more than a year before he reached the land of the Cimmerians, who dwell at the edge of the world. Traveling entertainers almost never came there—the land was so remote and empty—but Orpheus came, for he had learned that near there was an entrance to the land of the dead. It was a deaf man who showed him the way to the cave mouth, who could read in Orpheus's eyes the plaintive purpose of his journey. There, at the mouth of the cave, the dark floor sloped downward into blackness, then wound round and round deeper into night.

For days Orpheus walked in the darkness, stumbling and groping, aided only by the slope of the rocky floor, leading him almost unconscious ever downward. His legs seemed to move with their own will, freeing his mind to think in the darkness, to think, only one thought—Eurydice—to conjure up in his mind the memory of her face, her thighs, her breasts, the smell of her skin close to his. And then...

He heard the rushing water slapping against rocks in the distance echoing through the tunnel, and he knew at last he was near the River Styx, the watery boundary between the land of the living and the land of the dead.

At first Orpheus couldn't see him, since the figure was cowering behind a boat in what had become the dimmest of light. He was Charon, ferryman of ghosts. Even before Charon had seen Orpheus in the dark, he had heard his footsteps, so loud because those who had taken that path before had never made footfalls that could be heard, ghosts that they were.

Orpheus demanded passage and, because he was alive, Charon was too frightened to refuse. As Orpheus stepped into his rowboat, the hull sank deep into the waters of the Styx and some of the foul water lapped in, Charon cursing and muttering all the while—his ghostly passengers before had always been so light and had never caused the boat to sink into the river or caused him to push so hard upon the pole.

As Charon poled the boat through the clinging mist, it seemed to Orpheus he could smell the perfume Eurydice wore, and he urged Charon on. And then, seemingly before it had begun, the smooth passage was complete and the boat touched what had once been a far shore. Charon merely pointed a ghostly finger in the direction of a cavern and Orpheus, as though he had traveled that way once before, silently understood.

As he walked now, he could discern in the mist huddled clutches of human forms with only whispers for voices. Some of the figures seemed to point at him and, simultaneously, to step back in fear. At times he even thought he heard his name spoken, but it was hard to know. All fact, all reality, was sucked into the mist where it seemed to dissolve.

Few are tortured in the kingdom of Hades. It is not heaven or hell, but an in-between that, like the mist swirling and insubstantial, is everywhere. A hand sweeps through it and the mist returns, silently refilling the void.

On one side and then the other as Orpheus walked he could make out open spaces where individuals stood as though on stages, but stages with no audience before them and open on all sides. These were the special places of torture for those who had sinned against the gods: the sinners Sisyphus, Tityus, and Tantalus.

He could see Sisyphus straining in the dust to force the great boulder up the mound one inch at a time, only to slip and fall near the summit and see it tumble back down to the bottom once more, from which he had to—even as he had an eternity of times before—begin the upward push again. Orpheus recalled that in stories he had heard the mound was a great hill or mountain, but it was, it seems, far smaller, a mere conical mound of earth. And it occurred to him just for a moment that the mound resembled a breast and the round boulder a nipple and that, for all his straining, Sisyphus was mindless of where he was or what he was doing.

For his part, Tityus was writhing on the ground just as the poets had said, but not because he was bound by rope and stake with a vulture perpetually feasting on his liver, but rather because some unsatisfied and invisible torment ate away at his flesh, a hunger that could never be sated. Orpheus could see no fetters, but Tityus's torture seemed no less real for all of that or, in fact, even more terrible because its source was within, an enchainment from which he could never break free.

And Orpheus saw Tantalus standing, just as he heard, in a pool of water shaded by boughs hung with fruit. And each time he reached out a wind blew the boughs away. And each time he bent down for the water, its level receded. So much was true.

But the fruit and water were not as the poets had described them. Orpheus marveled how one could be driven by the lust for an apple so impoverished it looked rotten when fresh, ripening as it did in the darkness of Hades's kingdom. And he wondered at how Tantalus could be lured by the liquidity of water as sickeningly murky as that of the River Styx he had crossed. Or was it his hunger and thirst that made all things, even dead things, desirable that to the dispassionate eye of another might seem disgusting at best?

Suddenly in the midst of his reverie, thinking that all the poets had lied, that even Homer had been blind in unsuspected ways, having never seen (or dared to candidly report) the banal truth behind the legends generations had revered, Orpheus suddenly stumbled over his own feet and, turning as he got up, saw in the darkness to his right the glint of gilded ebony, the glistening shapes of a throne's polished legs and arms, two thrones in fact, and on those thrones the forms of two figures seated, and he realized—a chill seizing his whole body—that he was standing before the very sovereigns of death, dread Hades, master of all ghosts, and his dread regent Persephone.

Hades was first to speak, but even as the words came from his mouth, Orpheus continued to look at Persephone. Her face was turned away and covered by a darkness that hid almost every feature. Strands of hair fell across her cheek.

"The dead, the *dead*," Hades said emphatically as though to recapture his attention, "*cannot* be returned. Your journey, exceptional as it is, is simply useless. Go now the way you came!"

All this time Persephone's face was still turned away from Orpheus. And Hades's voice was strangely familiar, not unlike his own.

"And if my journey *is* useless, Hades," Orpheus answered him, "why is it that I was allowed to come? Though countless souls made this journey before, none was alive as am I. I have dreamed to come here to seek the return of the one I love, to plead with you for the life of Eurydice. Some day you will have her back. All must ultimately yield to your sovereign power. Let her live with me for but a short time. Any life, however long, would surely be short if measured against the eternity our souls must endure here in your kingdom once we die. Can you deny me this small favor?"

"This is *my* kingdom, and I can deny whatever I wish," the god coldly replied. "But that object you are holding, what is that?"

As Hades asked, Orpheus looked at his hand and saw there the lyre that he had played so long ago when Eurydice had lived. And, now, strangely it was in his hand once again.

"You are a musician, are you not?" Hades asked. "There is little music here. Before you return, play for us."

Only then did Orpheus see the queen's face, still hidden in the shadows, turn toward him slightly, and he saw her hand move. It was then that he began to play, playing and singing not of the Eurydice he loved, but of the world she had surrendered in death, the world she left behind, sunlit and warm, verdant and flowering, the world that autumn had only now begun to touch. He sang of harvests abandoned, of youth lost, of promises left unfulfilled.

And when he was done, and the last note played, he could see tears rolling down her cheek, Persephone's cheek, queen of death who each summer's end surrendered summer to enter the dark world of her consort. She turned to King Hades, and he too saw the tears that fell from eyes that had once known endless summer, but now saw it needlessly die each year.

Hades then spoke. "I will make this exception," he said. "You may have Eurydice back again—but with one condition. To return to the region of light she must walk behind you as you lead the way. You must never look back as you walk or, if you do, she will surely vanish forever. She is behind you now. Now go!"

Orpheus did not know if he should trust Hades, but he had no choice. He walked, doubting Eurydice was behind him. He strained to hear her footsteps, but could not. Nor could he speak with her, for she was still a ghost and could not answer. He stepped slowly, fearing she would lose sight of him in the darkness, wondering in fact if she was still there, if she had even been there at the start. Knowing nothing else to do, Orpheus sang, sang the songs he had once sung to her while she was alive, now haltingly for he feared she was not there to hear.

Finally in the distance he could make out the figure of Charon, ferryman of the dead. He had already seen Orpheus and, as Orpheus drew nearer, did not even look up. But why did he not show surprise at seeing Eurydice, a ghost about to make an escape from the realm of the dead? Was she in fact not there? Had Orpheus's voice and his love not been enough to lead her back to life?

He turned. He had to turn, to know. And he saw her again, her eyes looking into his, her hand now reaching out. He stretched out his own hand to hers, to grasp it and take her to the boat. But even as he did, she seemed to draw away or be drawn back against her will into the darkness they had left.

Orpheus cried out, plunging his hand into the darkness to reach her own, crying out her name, but it was too late. Too late to save her. Too late to be free. He had learned what we all must learn, that wishing for something we have lost is not enough to save it, even if we wish with all our heart and might.

The Sacrifice of Alcestis

The story of Alcestis is a story of self-sacrifice, the story of a woman who so loved her husband that she surrendered her life for his. But it is also the story of Admetus, her husband, who accepted the gift she gave.

When the story opens (Euripides dramatized this tale), the god Apollo bestowed a special blessing upon Admetus. On the day he was fated to die, he could continue to live, provided he found another to willingly take his place and die for him. All had refused, even his father and mother. Only his wife, Alcestis, had agreed. Death now made his appearance to claim his victim.

On her deathbed, Alcestis asks Admetus to swear he will not marry another once she has died, and he agrees, wishing he had the powers of Orpheus to lead her back from Hades's realm.

As the funeral is taking place, an unexpected guest arrives at the palace, none other than Hercules. Not wanting to burden his guest with his own grief, Admetus does not tell Hercules that Alcestis is dead. But Hercules finds out later and formulates a plan; he will catch up with Death and wrestle him for Alcestis's soul.

Overpowering Death at her tomb, Hercules frees Alcestis and returns with her to Admetus's palace, her face covered in a veil.

In the meantime, Admetus has recognized what a coward he was to let another die for him. He has saved his life, he realizes, but at the price of his honor. It is as though he is already dead.

Just then Hercules appears, the veiled woman in train. "I won her in a wrestling match," Hercules says. "Keep her 'til I return."

After first refusing, Admetus takes her hand and later, glimpsing her face, realizes it is Alcestis, miraculously home. He is overjoyed and thanks Hercules for being his savior. Alcestis, however, is silent; she cannot speak until three days more have passed and the stain of death is washed away.

But Admetus's stain will never be washed away. He let another die in his stead, and, despite his promise to his dying wife, he took another woman into his home on the very day of her funeral.

The problem with sin, for the Greeks, was that it could never be fully washed away. Like tragedy itself, it is interwoven with our character. We can no more escape it and be free than we can escape ourselves.

Mortal Lessons

These stories teach us that love and death are intertwined, and we can only be free when we have accepted both. Rather than celebrating the triumph over death, these myths underscore how rare such triumph is. Recognizing this, the ancient Greeks valued their freedom all the more during their lifetimes. The recognition of death's finality can therefore lead us to live our lives with greater passion and intensity. Ironically, death's greatest gift can be the liberating realization of life's value.

Loving Freedom

One of the greatest legacies bequeathed to us by the ancient Greeks is the gift of democracy. But it is a gift easily lost, for the values of a democracy can be perverted by popular will until democracy itself is but an empty shell.

To love freedom means to protect it, but the blessings of freedom, like democracy itself, are easily surrendered. Like air, the freedom we breathe tends to be taken for granted until the level of pollutants rises so high that emergency action is called for, action that may come too late.

The freedom of a state, of course, is simply a macrocosmic version of the freedom of the individual. To be free is to be free to do everything or nothing. As the Greeks understood, freedom is not self-justifying, but is merely a condition; it is what we do with it that counts. Thus the freedom we enjoy as individuals comes with an implicit obligation, the obligation to exercise it responsibly for our own benefit and the benefit of others.

We are free to be civilized Lapiths, or free to be barbaric Centaurs. The choice is ours. To make the love of freedom a part of our daily lives, we must recognize how precious a thing it is and what an opportunity it gives us to secure personal fulfillment, and, at the same time, contribute to others' lives.

CHAPTER 8

THE EIGHTH PILLAR
INDIVIDUALISM

The eighth, and final, pillar of Greek wisdom is individualism. Individualism means having pride in our uniqueness as human beings and in our personal capacity to achieve great things. Unless we care about our fulfillment as individuals, the full meaning of freedom will never be understood.

Individual and State

Unlike early civilizations of the ancient Near East, which viewed the individual as subservient to the state, the civilization of the ancient Greeks gave the individual preeminence. The chief virtues in Egypt and Mesopotamia were obedience and humility; in Greece the chief virtues were pride and self-realization.

The importance of the individual is evident in the earliest works of Greek literature, like Homer's *The Iliad* and *The Odyssey*, where the individual hero is the epic poet's subject. To a people who lacked God-given scripture, these epic poems endured for centuries as sources of spiritual guidance and humanistic inspiration long after the feudal age they described had vanished into history. Greek children learned these poems by heart and carried them in their hearts as they pursued adult life.

The importance the Greeks assigned to the individual is also manifest in the institution of democracy, a Greek invention. The structure of democracy is founded upon faith in individual responsibility and confidence in individual judgment. Trial by a jury of one's peers is another Greek invention founded upon the same premise (and, incidentally, formulated almost two thousand years before a similar concept in England's Magna Carta).

But prizing the individual did not mean despising the state. The ancient Greeks took citizenship seriously because they held the concept of community in high esteem, revered its laws as a child respects its parents, and acknowledged the community as the nurturer of the self. Anyone who failed to do so was an *idiotés*, a "person concerned only about his own affairs," a Greek word from which, significantly, our own word "idiot" derives.

The Greek concept of individualism was, in fact, rooted in the history of the Greek community. The Greek word for a community was *polis* from which our word "politics" comes. A *polis* was a self-reliant and economically self-sufficient city-state, a city and the countryside surrounding it. It was the geography of Greece, made up of mountain-rimmed valleys and sea-girt islands that gave birth to the independent city-state system, as opposed to the flat, alluvial plains of Egypt and Mesopotamia, which fostered the rise of monolithic nations. Greece's geography thus critically shaped its social psychology.

A Land of Heroes

The Greek concept of the individual was not static, but dynamic. Humanism might be a given, but implied the pursuit of excellence as its justification and individualism as its example. Therefore the hero was a work in progress, continually striving, seeking, finding, and not yielding. To be sure, not all the Greeks *were* heroes, but they *had* heroes, individuals whose larger-than-life exploits roused them to be more than they would otherwise have been. Those heroes were not perfect; they all had flaws. But this is what made them believable, and captured the imagination. A civilization that has no heroes is impoverished, not because it has no past, but because it has no future.

If individualism played such a great role in Greek life, it is only natural to expect that it played a great role in Greek myth. And so it did. Mythic stories often speak of monsters and quests. The two are, of course, interrelated, as the Greeks well knew. To attain our goals we must triumph over our fears. Each hero needs a quest, not because he is already a hero, but because the quest makes him one. We need not worry, then, that we are not heroes. A hero is something we become.

The Dragon's Teeth

Cadmus, a prince from Phoenicia, traveled to Greece to search for his sister Europa, who had been kidnapped by the god Zeus.

Instructed by the oracle of Delphi to follow a cow and build a city where it lay down, Cadmus arrived at the future site of the city of Thebes. As Cadmus made ready to sacrifice the cow, he sent his men to a nearby spring to fetch water, not knowing that the spring was guarded by a dragon. The dragon killed Cadmus's men, and Cadmus in turn courageously slew the dragon. On Athena's advice he pulled out the dragon's teeth and sowed them like seeds in the ground. Suddenly, from each tooth sprang a fully armed warrior. Before the warriors could attack him, Cadmus threw stones in their midst. Each warrior, assuming he was being attacked by one of his fellows, drew his sword, and the soldiers ended up killing each other, all except five whom Cadmus then enlisted to help him found his new city.

The Eyes of Medusa

Though his father was the god Zeus, Perseus grew up as a poor fisherman after he and his mother were cast adrift upon the sea and washed ashore on a small island. When the king of the island demanded that Perseus's mother marry him, Perseus set off on a quest to protect his mother from the king's cruelty. His quest was to bring back the head of Medusa, a monster from whose hair serpents grew. Should you look into her eyes, she would turn you to stone.

As Perseus entered her lair, he spied statues of warriors with their swords upraised. Upon closer inspection, however, he discovered that they were not statues at all, but petrified men who had once tried to slay the monster and had been turned to stone by her penetrating gaze.

She sat with her back turned toward him. This was the chance he was waiting for. But if she heard him and turned, she would attack. Should her eyes meet his, he would instantly become another statue in Medusa's human museum.

Stealthily he crept up behind her, never looking at her directly, but instead watching her reflection on the polished surface of his metal shield. Now near enough, he raised his sword and swung down with all his might. With a crunch and whoosh the monster's head toppled from her shoulders and tumbled to the ground, the snakes writhing in their death agony until finally they hung motionless and limp.

Fearing to look into even the dead eyes of Medusa, Perseus averted his gaze as he reached down with his hand and grasped the head by its snaky hair, plopping it into a leather sack he had brought along for the occasion. When Perseus returned home, the king asked to see his "wedding present." Reaching into the sack, Perseus held it up, and his enemy turned instantly to stone.

Facing some monsters, it turns out, doesn't necessarily mean looking them straight in the eye. But with cunning and courage they can be slain none the less. Perseus fulfilled the courageous individualism latent within him by rising above his fears.

The Golden Fleece

For one hero, it wasn't a monster's head or a dragon's teeth, but a ram's fleece that was the prize. The hero's name was Jason, and he got his assignment from a wicked uncle who wanted him dead. The Golden Fleece hung from a sacred oak, and to get it Jason had to sail to the edge of the known world, enduring trials and temptation along the way.

To reach the land of Colchis, home of the Golden Fleece, Jason had to cross the Black Sea. To do so, he ordered a special ship built, called the Argo, named for Argus, its designer. But he still needed a crew ready for adventure. Answering his call were mythic figures such as Hercules, the musician Orpheus, Alcestis's husband Admetus, and Peleus, father of Achilles, a band collectively dubbed the Argonauts.

On the voyage to Colchis no obstacle involved more risk that the passage through the Symplagades, or "clashing rocks," a set of twin promontories that guarded the entrance to the Black Sea. The rocks were mobile and would crush anything that passed between them. Jason tried an experiment and let a dove fly through; the dove did so, minus a tail feather. If the dove could do it, he reasoned, the swift ship could do it to. With a hand from Athena it did, losing only the pennant from its stern.

Aeëtes, the king of Colchis, wasn't pleased by his unexpected guests because an oracle had warned him to beware of strangers. But Jason and the Argonauts found an ally in the king's daughter, Medea, who fell in love with Jason the moment she saw him.

Her father set out the rules. Jason must yoke a pair of fire-breathing oxen, plow a field, and sow it with the teeth of a dragon once slain by the hero Cadmus. The teeth were available; the catch was that armed soldiers would spring from the ground wherever the teeth were sown, soldiers who would then have to be killed. Naturally, Aeëtes assumed Jason would never pass the test, and Jason even had doubts of his own, but the task had to be completed.

Medea helped by providing a magic salve to protect his skin from the oxen's fiery breath. Jason in turn promised to take her with him and marry her if their plan proved a success.

Sure enough, Jason was able to withstand the fire. He wrestled the oxen to the ground and yoked them as required and then proceeded to sow the dragon's teeth. As predicted, a fully armed warrior arose from each seed. To confuse the battalion, however, Jason, like Cadmus before him, hurled a huge boulder into their midst. Each warrior assumed the other had thrown the rock, and so they fought one another to the death. Meanwhile, other warriors were beginning to sprout. Quickly, Jason weighed in with his sword and finished them off.

The Fleece was his; at least, it *would* have been had Aeëtes been cooperative. But the king suspected collusion, and Medea, fearing what her father might do next, decided to take Jason to the Fleece herself. The Fleece was guarded by a dragon, but Medea, ever the sorceress, used a magic potion and put it to sleep.

With the Golden Fleece in hand and Medea beside him, Jason boarded the Argo with his crew and set sail for home. The rest of the story you know from chapter 5. Jason eventually abandoned Medea and their children, and she took her bloody revenge.

The Failure of Success

Jason's story illustrates, as does every heroic tale, the merits of individualism, but it also points out its limitations. First of all, Jason could never have accomplished his mission without help—the help of the Argonauts, and especially the help of Medea. While heroes may seem like loners, what they achieve is rarely achieved alone. Think also of

Theseus and his conquest of the Labyrinth. Could he have ever escaped without Ariadne's thread?

Secondly, the story shows us what a self-defeating thing individualism can become if it turns into shallow self-centeredness. When Jason disregarded the sacrifices Medea had made for him, and callously exchanged her for a new wife to advance his career, he sealed his own doom.

Theseus had done much the same thing, abandoning Ariadne on a deserted island on his voyage back to Athens. With the Minotaur dead, he thought, he didn't need her anymore. But, preoccupied with his own success, he forgot to change the sails of his ship from black to white (the signal to his father that he was alive and well). Sighting the black sails and believing his son dead, Theseus's father committed suicide.

In short, a virtue carried to a selfish extreme becomes a vice. Of course, Achilles is the prime example, a man who became so consumed with his own needs and the gratification of his own ego that he lost the one human being, Patroclus, that he ever really loved. In the end, Achilles died a hollow man.

By cultivating our individualism, can each of us some day find the Golden Fleece? Not likely. After all, Jason's story is a myth, as was the Golden Fleece itself. But for each of us there *is* a "golden fleece" of sorts, a thing we long for and desire that we may someday attain through talent and drive. In pursuing such an objective, however, we must always bear in mind that true success is rarely achieved alone. To thread the Labyrinth or to shield our skin from fire, we may need another's love and help. And when we sail for home, the prize alone will be poor company.

The Reflection in the Pool

Individualism that leads to self-absorption can be fatal, as the myth of Narcissus shows. Narcissus was an extraordinarily handsome young man, loved and desired by many. But, like Hippolytus, he scorned their love and rejected their advances. It is said that a nymph named Echo once fell in love with him. Poor Echo had been punished by Hera. Unable to initiate a conversation, Echo could only repeat another's words. Once she saw Narcissus, she fell madly in love with him, but didn't know what to say.

Hearing her footsteps behind him in the woods, Narcissus called out, "Is anyone here?" "Here," answered Echo. "Then come to me," he said. "Come to me," she answered. As he approached, she stepped from behind the tree and ran to embrace him, but Narcissus pulled back and ordered her to leave. "Leave," she said and turned away sadly. The story says that she pined for Narcissus for such a long time that she grew faint, and her body disappeared, leaving only her echo behind.

As for Narcissus, he eventually died, the victim of a curse. "May you someday desire someone," cried a rejected lover, "as much as others have desired you."

It didn't take long for the curse to be fulfilled. One day walking through the woods, Narcissus came to a pool. Bending over to drink from its waters, he saw the face of a beautiful young man looking up at him from beneath its surface. As he drew closer, the young man drew closer to him; as Narcissus spoke, the young man seemed to speak, though Narcissus could not hear his words. Yet as Narcissus broke through the surface of the water with his outstretched hand, the face beneath disappeared. Narcissus lay beside the pool tormented, unable to satisfy his desire, rising to look once again, and falling back again in defeat, until he finally died.

When he had been born, his mother had asked an oracle if her son would live long. "Yes," the oracle had replied, "as long he doesn't know himself." Even self-knowledge can be fatal if carried to an extreme, a warning to each of us to beware of the narcissism lurking in the deep pool of our mind.

In fact, one of life's dangers is falling in love with who we are at the moment instead of who we can become. No amount of gazing into a crystal ball, or pool of water, can ever show us that "other us"; only time and growth can bring it forth if our passion for life endures.

Individualism and Isolation

In the most extreme and pure sense, to be an individual means to live a life apart from others, emotionally and even physically. For most of their history, such an idea was repugnant to the Greeks, who believed the full development of the self can only take place within the context of society. The Athenian statesman Pericles said as much in his famous Funeral Speech, but the principle can be documented as far back as Homer. One of the main reasons the Cyclops and his brethren were contemptible, the poet tells us, was that each man lived as a law unto himself: if the giants responded to their brother's cries when he was blinded, they most likely did so because he had disturbed their sleep rather than because they cared about his welfare.

There were exceptions, of course. In the Hellenistic Age the Cynic philosophers argued that a man can only find peace if he cuts himself off from his dependency on others and drops the baggage of social regulations and rules. But this was the exception. Individualism was a virtue, but most Greeks felt it shouldn't be carried to such an extreme. Offered the sensual company of a goddess and the promise of eternal youth, Ulysses was right to turn down the offer since it meant exiling himself from humanity and home. Homer would have readily agreed with John Donne, "No man is an island, entire of itself."

The Land of the Lotus-Eaters

But exile can be measured not only in space, but also in time. On their voyage home from Troy, Ulysses and the veterans under his command came to a foreign shore. After landing, Ulysses sent out a scouting party to make contact with the natives. However, when they failed to return, he went out himself with others to find them.

When Ulysses came upon the people who had disappeared, he found them happily sharing the hospitality of the natives, eating the fruit of a plant called the lotus. The plant was flowery and its fruit as sweet as honey.

When Ulysses commanded his men to return to their ships, they resisted, preferring to stay with their new friends and eat more lotus. They found it hard to remember why they had sailed in the first place and forgot the homes and families they had left behind. They even had difficulty remembering Ulysses's name. Seeing this, Ulysses immediately ordered them taken back to the ship by force, even though they protested fiercely, and tied them down to their rowing-benches to make sure they didn't jump overboard and swim back once the ships were under way.

The point of the story is that memory makes us human. Deprived of remembrance we cease to be human, however pleasant the forgetting. Memory ties us to the world outside ourselves. Without it, our identity— and our individuality—is irrevocably diminished. Had Ulysses's men stayed in the Land of the Lotus-Eaters, they would have forgotten who they were. Remembering the past, struggling in the present, and working toward the future is fundamental to the durability of civilization, even as it is essential to the wholeness of our lives.

The Sacrifice of Prometheus

Of all those who stood for individualism, none paid a higher price than the god Prometheus. According to the story, Zeus, the king of the gods, became angry at the human race and decided to punish it by depriving it of the fire it had used to cook and keep warm.

Prometheus had originally fashioned man out of clay and still felt affection for his creation. So he decided to help the human race by stealing fire from heaven. This he did by hiding it in the hollow of a reed and transporting it to Earth.

When Zeus learned what Prometheus had done in secret, he was enraged all the more and decided to inflict his vengeance on mankind's benefactor. He had Prometheus arrested, and chained him eternally to the rocky face of a barren and remote mountain. Then Zeus sent his pet bird, the eagle, to tear into Prometheus's liver by day, while the organ grew back at night so it could be attacked again the next morning. For a thousand years this torment went on until Zeus finally relented.

In his defiance of tyranny, Prometheus stands as the ultimate symbol of individualism, but from his supreme sacrifice we see that individualism is not synonymous with selfishness. The courageous individual can be society's savior.

Repeatedly, the heroes of ancient Greece faced terror, and repeatedly triumphed over it by drawing upon their inner resources. With physical strength and intelligence, they defeated the monsters that stood in their path, thereby defending not only themselves, but civilization.

The Education of Alexander

Alexander wasn't born "the Great"; he *became* great. How did it happen? The answer is education, and the education of Alexander can be instructive. It can show us how to realize our potential as individuals.

Alexander's character was shaped by his parents, his teachers, and myth. Alexander was born in Macedonia in 356 B.C. His father was Macedonia's king, a rough-hewn warrior named Philip. Alexander's father became his role model: a leader of men and a conqueror of nations, who forged a kingdom out of Greece in the aftermath of the war between Sparta and Athens. Unlike his pragmatic father, Alexander's mother, Olympias, had a mystic temperament. She told her son that Zeus, not Philip, was his real father, and the seed of divinity implanted in the young Alexander's mind led him to dream even larger dreams than he would have otherwise dreamt.

Knowing that his son would succeed him (the history of Macedonian kingship was scarred by multiple assassinations), Philip determined to give his son an education that would fully prepare him for the leadership of Greece. Macedonia was a semi-barbarous country in the eyes of the classical Greeks who lived to the south, and a country not known for high culture. Therefore, Alexander's tutor would have his work cut out for him. Philip sent for Aristotle, a man who had been born in Macedonia and had become a philosopher and Plato's most famous pupil. Aristotle schooled Alexander in the literature and wisdom of Greece, teaching him the very same principles that you have learned and the heroic myths you have read.

Two mythic figures came to stand out in Alexander's growing mind: Hercules and Achilles. Each had attained everlasting fame through super-human efforts. By being the son of Zeus, Hercules was, in a sense, Alexander's half-brother. Alexander also claimed descent from Aeacus, the ancestor of Achilles. Thus his mythic role models were virtual members of his family. When Alexander went to war, it is said he slept with two objects under his pillow: a dagger and a copy of *The Iliad*, Achilles's tale. When he ruled as king, Alexander issued coins bearing his heroic likeness, wearing the lion-skin cap Hercules wore after slaying the Nemean Lion. Alexander's character was thus shaped by his upbringing, by a father who served as a role model, by a mother who taught him to dream, and by a teacher who instilled in him the inspiring values of a higher culture.

We can ask no less of ourselves as parents, or of our schools. Our children may not have famous forebears or legendary ancestors, but we can teach them by example, help them to dream, and instill in them the guiding principles of a purposeful life. And though as adults we may lack an Aristotle to school us, we can still avail ourselves of his wisdom and that of his ancient peers. Their voices are as near as the nearest library or bookstore. They are there every day, patiently waiting for us to hire them, and to collaborate with us in the great adventure that is the life of the mind.

Alexander was not perfect. He aimed too high, drove himself too hard, and failed in his greatest dream. But that is only proof that he was Greek in spirit, and human like ourselves. If we aim too low, we will never hit the mark. If we drive too slow, we may never reach our destination. And if we dream too small, we will die as small as our dreams.

Alexander saw himself as a rational individual. He drank in freedom and was consumed by curiosity. He sought self-knowledge by testing his limits through the pursuit of excellence. And, in the process, he fulfilled his humanity. His name in Greek aptly meant "defender of man."

Long after his death his name lives on in the name of every person called Alexander or Alexandra. But his name also lives on in myth, because Alexander the man became Alexander the legend.

Legends of Alexander

Riding a Shadow

Alexander's father once owned a high-spirited horse that no one could ride. Unable to break it, Philip ordered the horse destroyed.

Alexander then appealed to his father, begging that he be given the chance to tame the wild stallion. Young Alexander had seen what no one else had: the horse was frightened by its own shadow.

He kept the stallion's face pointed to the sun, whispering gently and gaining its confidence, until he could finally mount and ride it. The spirited horse became his, and was appropriately named Bucephalus ("bull-headed"). Alexander was the only one ever to ride Bucephalus and the steed carried him on his campaigns across the world. When Bucephalus died of old age on the Indian frontier, Alexander grieved and buried his loyal companion with great ceremony, founding a city beside its grave, which he named Bucephalia.

A Knot Untied

For some, even being king is not enough. It is said that young Alexander wept in Macedonia's royal palace every time he learned that his father had won another victory—Alexander feared that when he grew up there would be no more worlds left for him to conquer.

And so upon his father's death, in order to have a proper challenge by which to prove his worth, he marched against the Persian Empire, the largest empire the world had ever known. He vanquished it and drove on to India with his army, and might have gone on even to China had his men not threatened mutiny because they ached for home.

But Alexander ached for something he could never have or ever find. He ached for more than there was, more than *he* was, drunk as he was with the wine of becoming. Before he burned the palace at Persepolis, capital of the Persian kings, he had already forced the Delphic oracle to reveal to him his future glory, and had visited the ruins of Troy where he paid homage to Achilles's grave.

In the land of Lydia at the city of Gordion, Alexander was shown a knot, and was told that whoever could unloosen it would become the world's master. The knot was not one but many, all twisted and intertwined in a tight labyrinth of stout rope. For decades, many had tugged and pulled at it and failed. Alexander contemplated the Gordion knot for a moment, and in an instant slashed it in two with his sword. Some problems are not to be tugged at or pulled; they demand a bolder stroke.

The Emptiness of Power

Long before he left Greece on his mission, Alexander had sought out the philosopher Diogenes, a Cynic who lived in deliberate poverty because he preferred to depend on no one, believing instead that he who has less is more free.

Alexander found Diogenes sitting in a large broken urn, his makeshift home. Alexander courteously approached, and, as a king, politely asked the old man, "Is there anything I can do for you?"

Looking up, Diogenes snapped, "Yes, a small favor. Step out of my sunlight." The men in Alexander's retinue immediately laughed at the poor man's crude stupidity, but Alexander did not.

"Were I not Alexander," he said, "I would want to be Diogenes." He knew that power by itself can be emptier than a barrel, and darker if there is no sunlight to warm it.

Desert and Death

After he had finally defeated the king of the Persians, Alexander came to Egypt to liberate it from the hand of the Persians. But Alexander also came out of curiosity, to see this most ancient of lands. He made a point to travel far into the western desert to the oasis of Siwa where there was an oracle of Amun, whom the Greeks identified with Zeus.

When Alexander appeared before the oracle, the oracle chose to address him not in Egyptian, but in Greek. Yet being unfamiliar with the Greek tongue, he mistakenly called him *pai Dios* ("son of Zeus") instead of *paidios* ("my child"). The mistake only confirmed what Alexander already knew in his heart: his real father was not Philip of Macedonia, but Zeus himself.

Some claim the oracle said what he did deliberately to ingratiate himself with the conqueror. We will never know. What we do know is that in the end, Alexander proved he was mortal. He died of fever in his thirty-second year, leaving his empire for his generals to carve up. He had marched across a world three thousand miles wide, planting cities like seeds to absorb the light of the East and radiate the light of Greece. One of these cities was Egypt's Alexandria, which still bears his name.

Near the palace of his successors, the Ptolemies, stood his tomb. Inside was the golden casket in which his corpse was laid, brought there after he died in Babylon. It was his wish that he be buried in Egypt, a land that holds in her bosom the bodies of so many kings and their unspent dreams.

The Glass Submarine

Long after Alexander died, his memory lived on in the literary imagination of the West. One story made him the captain of an undersea submersible. It was made of glass for easier observation and was lowered by a chain from a rowboat topside. According to the story, Alexander had three passengers on board—a rooster, a dog, and a cat. The rooster was there because its crowing could help Alexander determine when a new day had dawned in the dark depths of the sea. The dog was there because of the belief that its breath could purify the air inside the cabin. And the cat was there because it had nine lives; in the event of an emergency, Alexander had merely to hold its tail and he would surface and be saved.

As fantastic as this tale is, it expresses something Alexander the Great and the Greek people believed in—it is our duty to explore the unknown. Only by taking risks can we grow as individuals.

Becoming an Individual

I've titled this section "*Becoming* an Individual" rather than "*Being* an Individual" because according to the Greeks, individuality is not a numerical distinction, but is a state of mind. Our individuality is to be measured by the degree to which we strive to be unique rather than by the degree to which we are alone.

Of course, marching to a different drummer may separate us from the parade. But that is as it should be. There was, the Greeks believed, an inevitable tension between the individual and the group. Resistance to arbitrary authority was for them a persistent literary theme and, at times, a painful historical fact. There was always a price to be paid for radical individualism. Often, as in the cases of Antigone and Socrates, it was death; sometimes, as in the cases of Prometheus and Achilles, it was far worse. But nothing, as the Greeks saw it, came without a price. And individualism, as an ideal, was worth the price because without it society itself was worthless.

How can we apply this principle to our everyday lives? The answer is obvious and, regrettably, so is the price—even today.

If you have bought or borrowed this book, and if you have read as far as this chapter, you are without doubt an individual. Not only am I gratified, but the ghosts of the Greeks are, too. You have warmed their hearts for so long chilled by the isolation of Hades.

Homer tells us that when the voyager Ulysses met the ghost of Achilles in Hades (Ulysses was just passing through), Ulysses complimented him on the prestige he enjoyed among the dead. Achilles then answered coldly, "I'd rather be the poorest slave of the poorest peasant on Earth than be king among the dead." Life on any terms, Achilles had come to see, was preferable to all the posthumous honors he could get. Only when Ulysses told him about Achilles's son Neoptolemus—a warrior like his father and the bravest of the brave, always pursuing excellence—did Achilles's chest swell with pride.

If you are even now striving in your life to be an individual, relishing freedom and restless in curiosity, plying reason to gain self-knowledge, tempering the drive to excel with moderation, and thus fulfilling the promise of your humanity, you too make Achilles proud and all his company who, across the centuries, lived "to strive, to seek, to find, and not to yield."

CHAPTER 9

OBSTACLES ALONG THE WAY

Every Greek hero who completed an adventure faced obstacles along the way. In fact, if the obstacles hadn't existed, by definition the adventure wouldn't have been heroic. It's only natural, then, to expect that there will be obstacles in our path, especially if the adventure we are on could change our lives.

Our adventure, in effect, is a journey not through space but through time, a journey that challenges us to retrieve the values of a distant past and make them an integral part of the present.

Think of it as a transplant operation of a very experimental type. We will be transplanting into a modern body the spirit of an ancient world. Whether the transplant is effective will depend upon the compatibility of the recipient and the donor. That you have cared enough to learn about the Greek heart tells me you are a suitable candidate to receive that organ. As for the donor, no more willing donor could be found. The Greeks, after all, longed to transcend death: through art, through literature, and through the memory of posterity. The operation can proceed.

But with every surgery there are risks. To minimize them, the operating room must be clean, the surgical instruments sterile, the hands of the surgeon scrubbed—all to prevent infection.

But the spiritual operation we are to perform cannot take place in a germ-free environment. Every patient is a part of his society, and there are social contaminants that will be hard to purge.

Contemporary society is radically different from the society of ancient Greece.

To understand how far we are removed from the world of ancient Greece, we need to focus on some of modern society's most distinctive features. To be sure, these features do not constitute the whole of what we would call our world. But, nevertheless, they require our attention because of what they imply about the feasibility and long-term success of the value-transfer we propose.

The Power of Technology

In the world of the Greeks, technology was not the force it is today, but it was still a part of their everyday lives. The ancient Greeks even had a god of technology. His name was Hephaestus, and Greek myth describes him as a lame metalsmith. He fashioned the shield that Achilles carried into battle to avenge his friend's death. Homer tells us Hephaestus (later known to the Romans as Vulcan) even had a set of voice-activated, robotic bellows to keep his melting-pots hot.

If Hephaestus was the divine patron of blacksmiths, Prometheus was the archetypal potter, whose most famous work was man himself, whom he shaped out of clay. The Greeks, moreover, attributed to Prometheus all the arts and sciences that made civilization possible.

As for woman, she was Hephaestus's work, designed to punish mankind. On Zeus's order, Hephaestus took clay and sculpted the first woman. When she arrived on Earth, she brought with her a special jar or box containing every human ill, which she released for the first time when she lifted the lid. She bore the euphemistic name Pandora ("all-gifted") and with her arrival, says Greek myth, man's troubles began.

The creative imagination of the Greeks also endowed their gods with superhuman powers that featured what we might call advanced technology. Hermes, the divine messenger, could fly through the air at high speed on winged sandals, and Zeus was armed with a ballistic missile of sorts, his fiery thunderbolt.

Under very special circumstances even a human could fly, as the inventor Daedalus proved. And the mythical Phaeacians, who brought Ulysses home to Ithaca, sailed in ships that could skim across the waves at more than one hundred miles per hour.

But these were exceptional powers attributed to mythical or divine figures, not ordinary men. Today, however, we possess the powers of the ancient gods—the power to streak across the sky in a jet, to obliterate a city with a nuclear thunderbolt, or to manipulate the very substance of life by engineering DNA.

These powers have made us stronger, but, regrettably, not wiser. We lack the Delphic vision to adequately foresee the consequences of our acts and the emotional restraint to control them. The resources at our disposal invite us to commit acts of hubris on a cosmic scale never before conceived. In addition, our inventiveness has give us a bottomless Pandora's box of so-called labor-saving devices that unfortunately seem only to complicate our lives more. The more our everyday existence becomes more harried and artificial, the more insulated we become from the rhythms of nature that could restore us. Without doubt, life in ancient Greece was simpler, and even primitive, by contemporary Western standards.

In general, Greece was an agrarian society, and her cities were small. Transportation was by foot, ox-cart, or sailboat; communication was almost entirely by word of mouth. There were no traffic jams because there was no traffic. There were no pagers or answering machines, no voice mail or email; in fact, there was no mail at all. There was no telemarketing because there was only one marketplace and that was in the center of town. There was no advertising, since there were no newspapers or magazines; there were no commercials, since there was no radio or TV. Work really began only when the sun rose, and basically had to end when it set, and, except for the occasional sun-dial or water-clock, there were no machines to measure it by. Almost all products were made by hand from natural materials, and the only available fuels were olive oil or wood.

It was precisely because of the absence of a synthetic world that Greek life could be more authentic. The absence of artificial distractions permitted the mind to focus, and the scarcity of complexity let the most essential issues stand out. Life was lived closer to nature, and, if physically harder because of that, was more comprehensible in its purposes and in its limitations. In short, human life was lived on a more human scale.

When it was the occasion for communal rejoicing, festivals were held. In classical Athens, dramatic entertainment was featured only twice a year, when a single theater served as the public venue. Entertainment did not, as it does today, constantly saturate the consciousness or assault the eye and ear with hyperstimulation. Indeed, no culture in the history of the world has been so incessantly amused as ours, or so persistently deprived of the chance for deep thought. Unlike the problem faced by the prisoner in Plato's cave, our problem today is not too little light, but too much, a light so glaring that we cannot see what is real.

By its basic character, then, the cultural environment of ancient Greece fostered the rise of humanism and the growth of humane principles complementary to it. Of course, many other cultures have been marked by simplicity and yet have not gone on to produce a Socrates or an Alexander the Great. Surely some other factors must have contributed to the formation of the Greeks' core values: an abundance of critical resources, a turn of history, a sense of national or civic pride, even a lucky roll of the genetic dice. But whatever those other factors were, the psychological landscape of Greece was not hostile to humanly centered beliefs, but was fertile enough to let them take root, unlike the technological terrain we inhabit today.

The Lure of Affluence

In inhibiting the adoption of Greek values, present-day affluence is as potent a deterrent as technology. Today, we have far more things than the ancient Greeks ever had, but the superabundance of those very things keep us from appreciating what the Greeks readily understood. Material possessions tend to crowd out the spiritual; ease and pleasure create a harder life for the mind. As simulated experience and synthetic gratification overwhelm our senses, the notion of a soul becomes more and more incomprehensible. By appealing to those senses, a materialistic environment makes us forget that we are more than our nerve endings, more than just consumers waiting to consume.

Ulysses confronted this danger in the Land of the Lotus-Eaters and pulled his men away before they surrendered their identity. Later, arriving on Circe's island, and welcomed by the enchantress, his men obeyed their appetites and filled their faces with food, only to be transformed by her magic wand into the carnal swine they were. Greek storytellers well understood the power of the appetite, and how it can transform us into creatures less noble than we are. In his book *The Classical Tradition*, Gilbert Highet commented eloquently on this danger. He wrote:

> Many of us misunderstand civilization. We live in a materialistic world. Most of us think incessantly about making money, or about gaining power—expressed in material terms—for one group or one nation, or about redistributing wealth between

> classes, countries, or continents. Nevertheless, civilization is not chiefly concerned with money, or power, or possessions. It is concerned with the human mind. The richest state in the world, or a world-society of unlimited wealth and comfort, even although every single one of its members had all the food and clothing and machines and material possessions he could possibly use, would still not be a civilization. It would be what Plato called "a city of swine," eating, drinking, mating, and sleeping until they died.

Being human, the Greeks were tempted by materialism too, especially in the affluent days of the Golden Age. In those pragmatic days, the Sophists taught the secret of success—do not have fixed ethical values at all. But the writers of tragedy knew the risks of moral blindness and the perils of success. Nemesis was always waiting in the wings. In the plays of Sophocles, a recurrent character is Tiresias, a prophet who was physically blind but could spiritually see what others, despite their eyes, could not.

There was also a danger in getting what you wish for, as the myths of Greece revealed. Romanced by a lover who told her he was really Zeus in disguise, Semele asked him to grant her a wish to prove his divinity. When Zeus consented, Semele asked him to appear to her in the same form that he used when he made love to Hera, his wife. Forced to comply, Zeus appeared to Semele in all his heavenly radiance, and burnt poor Semele to a crisp.

In another tale, Eos, the goddess of the dawn, begged Zeus to make her mortal lover immortal. Unfortunately, Eos lacked the foresight to ask for eternal youth. As a result, her lover Tithonus lived on, but grew older and more decrepit in bed until he finally turned into a shrunken, chirping cicada.

A third story of wish fulfillment gone awry is the most famous, the myth of King Midas. Granted a single wish by the god Dionysus, Midas wished for a golden touch. His wish was granted, much to his regret, because everything he touched then turned instantly to gold, including the food and drink he held in his hands. And when he embraced his beloved daughter, she too was turned into solid gold and died. Midas prayed for deliverance, which fortunately was granted. By bathing in a river, his golden touch was washed away.

Like the other stories, the myth of Midas teaches us to be careful before we wish. Our wish just might come true in a way we never anticipated. Midas's story, moreover, teaches us that money is not everything in life, and that great wealth can come at a terribly high price. Human beings, of course, have always aspired to a better life. The trick, as always, is to define what "better" really means.

The Effect of Speed

Another hostile element we must consider is speed. The effects of speed are more insidious than those of technology or materialism because speed itself is less visible though its effects are far-reaching.

People speak of "killing time"—when they're waiting for something to happen, when there's nothing else worth doing 'til then. They use up useless time by "killing" it. They are the killers; time is the victim.

But things have changed. Today, we are the victims, and time the killer. Time is using *us* up. We have a chronic condition that warps our values, a malady more pernicious because it goes so deep.

As so often happens, our present condition was anticipated by the ancient Greeks. They saw into the essence of what it means, and will always mean, to be human. In one Greek myth, in the beginning there was female Earth (Gaea) and male Sky (Uranus). The Sky spread over

Earth and impregnated her, but later hated the repulsive progeny she bore, and demanded she keep them in her womb. In retaliation, Earth fashioned a sickle and gave it to her son Kronos, instructing him to hide in ambush and await his father's return. When the Sky came back and again spread over Earth, Kronos seized the god's genitalia and castrated him with the adamantine blade. Robbed of his sexual potency, the Sky ceased to be king, and Kronos took his place on the cosmic throne.

But Kronos proved to be as tyrannical as his father. Hearing he would someday be supplanted by one of his children, he swallowed each in turn as they were born. The next time his mate gave birth, she hid the baby, substituting for it a stone wrapped in swaddling clothes, a package that Kronos promptly and stupidly gulped down. When the actual baby, named Zeus, was grown, he deposed his father in fulfillment of the prophecy and became the universe's next king. Greek myth is thus indelibly impressed with twin images of divine Kronos: castrator of his father and devourer of his children.

The latter image was depicted with horrifying impact by the Spanish artist Goya, who in the last years of his life painted the so-called "Black Paintings" on the walls of his retreat outside Madrid. In the panel called *Saturn Devouring One of His Sons* (Saturn being the Roman name for Kronos), a wild-eyed, hairy brute chews on the arm of a decapitated corpse.

Kronos's name was spelled by the Greeks with a kappa or *k*. But there is another word in their language that sounds like it: *Chronos*, spelled with a chi or *ch*. Chronos is the Greek word for time, from which so many time-related words in English come, like chronology and chronicle. The closeness in sound between the two words led Greek thinkers to speculate about a possible connection in meaning between them. After all, just like the primordial god Kronos, time also existed at the beginning of the world. Furthermore, like Kronos, time consumed things. The sixth/fifth century B.C. Greek poet Simonides described Chronos as "all-conquering" and "sharp-toothed," "wearing everything away, even what is strongest."

The tale of Kronos—a son castrating his father, a father devouring his children—makes a frightening pair of myths. Fortunately for us, such a mythic god does not exist!

Unfortunately, *this* god *does* live. We have kept him alive, and each year he grows more powerful, energized by two forces: the power of technology and the lure of materialism, forces that have increasingly come to define our cultural existence.

As late as 1983, only 8 percent of American households had computers, but by 1997 the figure had risen to 43 percent. By 2000, 55 percent of Americans had Internet access, and, of those, 36 percent were spending at least five hours a week online. Three and one half million hand-held computers were sold in 2000, almost five times the number sold just two years before. In 2000, sales of PCs topped forty-nine million. Meanwhile, the speed of supercomputers was approaching four trillion calculations per second.

Cell phone use was also climbing, with more than one out of every four Americans always on call and never out of reach. But even so, the U.S. was far behind other cellular places like Portugal, Australia, Denmark, Israel, Italy, Iceland, Hong Kong, Sweden, Norway, and the leader, Finland, where 60 percent of the population today is receiver-to-ear.

The velocity of society can also be measured by the speed at which people eat. By the year 2000, Americans were spending $110 billion dollars on fast food, with one out of four adult Americans visiting a fast-food restaurant every day. The biggest employer, public or private, in America and the largest owner of retail property in the entire world became

McDonald's, with twenty-eight thousand restaurants worldwide in over 110 nations, and two thousand new locations opening every year.

Faster and faster run our lives, driven by 24/7 technologies that operate not at the slower speed of machines, but at the velocity of light, impelled by electrons that do not sleep and material desires that remain forever unsatisfied. We live in a hyperculture governed by the power of now and dominated by an artificial urgency that will not let us rest. We see ourselves as consumers, not recognizing it is we who are consumed.

The acceleration of American life is made clear by a series of surveys. Asked in 1965 if their lives were "rushed all the time," 25 percent of those who responded said yes. By 1975, the figure was 28 percent; by 1985, 32 percent; by 1992, 38 percent—a 50 percent increase over the first survey. Not just "rushed," but "rushed all the time." Rushed (as surveys showed) at work, and rushed at play, rushed in big cities, and rushed in small towns.

But stress is only half the problem. The other half, the more insidious half, is our adaptation to speed: the price we pay for going so fast, a price paid in the currency of the human mind. We have less patience, less time to reflect. We need balance in our lives, but have few opportunities to find it. There is less permanence to ground our lives in because everything has become transient. What is valued is what is fast and new, and all the other things—tradition and craftsmanship, commitment and love—the slow and beautiful things, the old and precious things, no longer have a place because they take too much time.

Inundated with a rushing flood of data, we grasp at information mistaking it for knowledge, and reach for knowledge, mistaking it for wisdom. Even when we try to relax, we immerse ourselves in a sea of surging stimuli. Many have come to like it, to revel in their electronic addiction. And why not, since it gratifies the endings of their nerves, a biological level so much more accessible than the soul and ever so less demanding. If today's intimacy is electronic, the wired life is also devoid of warmth.

And so Time devours his children, even the youngest for whom life has become too much too soon, hurried into adulthood before they can mature, swallowed almost as soon as they are born.

If Time's children are the future, Time's father must be the past. And just as Chronos is devouring the future, so is he castrating that past. Survey after survey shows how historical knowledge has been emasculated and dethroned. A decade ago, you could graduate from 88 percent of America's best colleges and universities without ever having had to take a course in history. Even today, not one of those institutions requires its students to take a course in American history.

This too is a consequence of speed. The faster we drive, the smaller the image of the past becomes in the rearview mirror of our consciousness. The more it is "now" that matters, the less "then" will count. Yet how can democracy survive if history is impotent to affect the decision-making of its citizens?

Kronos/Chronos will continue to castrate his father and devour his children. He lives. But he only lives because we let him. It is not time that is our enemy, but what have we made time into.

Can we, in the end, undo what we have created, we who have become like gods ourselves? The answer to this question will determine not only the outcome of the present, but the shape of all things to come.

Predicting the Future

What, then, is humanity's long-range forecast? For better or worse, we lack the powers of a Delphic oracle.

Some Greeks, like the peasant-poet Hesiod, saw no hope of progress, but instead an inevitable decline, not in material as much as in moral terms. Yet if Hesiod was a pessimist, he had certainly seen enough injustice and inhumanity in his life to make him one. For Hesiod, the history of the human race had begun in a Golden Age that degenerated into Silver and Bronze. Next came the Ages of Heroes that Homer described. But now it was the Iron Age, worst of all, a corrupt age in which mankind would be abandoned to its own worst vices.

Were Hesiod surveying our own society through his ancient and pessimistic eyes, he would probably say we were further proof of his theory. Under the influence of technology, we have absorbed the insensate regimen of the machine into our hearts, substituting dehumanization for humanism. Under the influence of materialism, we have replaced the pursuit of excellence with the pursuit of money. In place of the practice of moderation, we have installed the practice of mediocrity; in place of self-knowledge, self-gratification; in the place of rationalism, rationalization; instead of restless curiosity, the invasion of privacy; instead of the love of freedom, the love of license; instead of individualism, self-centeredness.

Even if Hesiod spoke, few would listen. He would simply be dismissed as another hysterical Cassandra. Cassandra was sexually desired by Apollo, but had asked the god for a gift first: the ability to predict the future. But, once given the gift, she rejected her heavenly suitor. Apollo did not renege; he just added a stipulation. Whatever Cassandra predicted no one would believe. And so, as the story goes, she warned her fellow Trojans that Troy would fall, but her warnings were ignored.

Is *our* society heading for disaster? Or is that just Cassandra raving again?

In actuality, it probably is not the dramatic end of our society we should fear as much as its slow degeneration, so slow that it goes without notice, so slow that the unawakened soul continues to lie asleep. Yet at all times the power resides in every individual to awake. All we need to do is will it. And if we cannot "save the world," at least we can save ourselves and those we love.

Greek mythology tells us that once, out of anger at mankind for its sinfulness, Zeus decided to destroy the human race with a flood. Only two people were permitted to survive: a man named Deucalion and his wife, Pyrrha. When the waters of the flood receded, they were instructed to throw the bones of their mother over their shoulders. At first, they didn't understand, but then they remembered that their mother was Earth, and her "bones" were the stones around them. Bending down, they picked up some stones and threw them over their shoulders. As the stones fell to the ground, the ones Deucalion had thrown magically morphed into men, and ones Pyrrha threw, into women. Earth was repopulated with a purer race. So it may happen again someday, one man, one woman at a time, until a new race, and a new Golden Age, is born.

CHAPTER 10

CLIMBING OTHER MOUNTAINS

The ancient Mediterranean world was wider than the land of Greece. To the west lay Italy and the civilization of ancient Rome, to the east, the fabled lands of the Bible. So, if you're eager, there's more spiritual climbing to do.

The Legends of Rome

Like the Greeks, the Romans had their myths but, being a less imaginative folk, borrowed most of their myths from their Hellenic cousins. Ironically, it was the Roman poet Ovid who gave many of these Greek myths their most stylish treatment. In fact, his *Metamorphoses* became one of the world's greatest literary classics, inspiring later writers and artists.

The native myths of the Romans, however, are very different from those of the Greeks, as are the values they embody. Because of their ethnic and nationalistic slant, Roman myths reveal the unique principles by which the Romans lived. Together, these principles point to a definition of character very different from the one the Greeks lived by. As a result, examining the myths of Rome can give us a broader perspective on what it can mean to be human.

The Trials of Aeneas

Lacking a heroic pedigree, the early Romans decided to borrow one from Greece by tracing the origins of Rome to the Trojan War. The Roman poet Vergil told the story best in his patriotic epic, *The Aeneid*. According to the story, Aeneas (for whom the story was named), was a heroic Trojan warrior and prince. When the Greeks began to loot and burn Troy, Aeneas instinctively wanted to fight and die in defense of his city. But Jupiter (the Roman equivalent of Zeus) had other plans for him. Instead, Aeneas was given a divine command to abandon the burning city, gather his family and as many survivors as he could find, and sail off in search of a new homeland. The "promised land" was to be Italy, and three centuries after Aeneas's landing a new nation would arise, a nation to whom Jupiter promised an empire without end. Before reaching Italy, however, Aeneas had to surmount multiple obstacles and resist personal temptations in order to attain his goal.

Shortly after leaving Troy, Aeneas and his band of refugees came to a settlement recently founded on the Greek coast by other survivors of Troy's fall. These survivors had built an exact, but miniature, replica of Troy, and invited Aeneas and his followers to join them. But Aeneas pressed on, believing, as Thomas Wolfe once wrote, "You can never go home again." It is forward we must go.

Later, Aeneas and his people landed on the coast of North Africa near the city of Carthage. Dido, the widowed queen of Carthage, fell in love with Aeneas and offered him half her kingdom. But Aeneas was compelled to fulfill his destiny, even though it meant rejecting a passionate woman's love.

On the island of Sicily, the old and timid Trojans were left behind in order that the young and bold could sail on to the Italian mainland. Indeed, it was the old members of Aeneas's band who urged this radical step to ensure that only those who could fight for the future would go on. Like Janus, the Roman god of two faces, the Romans looked back to the past for wisdom, but looked forward to the future for success.

The Founding of Rome

Three centuries later, just as Jupiter had promised, the Roman nation was ready to be born. As the Roman historian Livy tells the tale, a noble named Amulius seized the throne of Alba Longa (a central Italian city) from his brother Numitor, the rightful king. To make sure that Numitor would have no male heirs, Amulius banished Numitor's daughter to a nunnery. But Mars, the Roman god of war, had other ideas. He visited the young woman in her convent and had sex with her. When her wicked uncle Amulius learned she had given birth to twin boys, he decided to eliminate them by putting the babies in a reed basket and setting them adrift in the River Tiber. As it turned out, the basket washed ashore on one of the river's banks. Hearing their cries, a female wolf dragged the basket to her lair on the Palatine Hill and nursed the infants with her own milk.

Later, the boys were adopted by a passing shepherd and learned of their true origin. Grown to manhood, they returned to Alba Longa and led a revolution that deposed Amulius and put Numitor back on the throne. But after their work was done, the two headed back to the place where they had grown up, accompanied by young men from Alba Longa who thirsted for adventure. Each of the twins, Romulus and Remus, founded a city on one of the nearby hills. Choosing the Palatine, Romulus named his city for himself and called it Rome. But Remus became jealous, and Romulus slew him in a fit of rage.

Romulus and his men soon realized they had a problem: no women to help them populate their new community. Romulus solved the problem by declaring a holiday and inviting a neighboring tribe, the Sabines, to join the festivities. At a prearranged signal, Romulus and his men leaped out and each grabbed a woman, fighting off their men. Now that Romulus and his men had Sabine women, the propagation of the Roman race could begin.

The Roman Achievement

Beginning as a primitive village of peasant-farmers, Rome rose to become the political and military master of the Mediterranean world and one of the most glorious cities of the ancient world. This rise to power and wealth was largely a consequence of the Roman people expressing their most basic values. These values were already evident in their central myths.

In Aeneas we see a man characterized not by individualism and restless curiosity, or by the love of freedom, but rather by a respect for divine authority and unquestioning obedience. Individualism was not a hallmark of Roman character, but the willingness to subordinate one's own needs to the higher needs of destiny and the state was. The later Romans were not curious about who they were as men, but were self-confident and self-assured about their place in the world and their right to rule it by force. In their laws, as in their engineering and architecture, the Romans manifested not abstract rationalism, but applied organizational skills. In short, they were doers rather than thinkers. At the height of their empire, they pursued pleasure over excellence, and practiced excess over moderation. Fathered by the war-god Mars and nursed by a savage she-wolf, Romulus was the true father of the Romans.

America's founding fathers, who learned about independence and liberty from the democratic Greeks, absorbed a great deal also from the Romans, especially the dangers of dictatorial power. Accordingly, they crafted the Constitution to include appropriate checks and balances to protect the freedoms they had fought for during the Revolutionary War. In the mind of European thinkers, Rome also illustrated how materialism could corrupt morals, just as Greece illustrated the virtues of idealism.

But there are many positive things we can extract from the Roman experience, including lessons we can apply to our personal development. Responsible for Roman success were qualities of national character that are still worthy of admiration and imitation: an abiding respect for law, a willingness to sacrifice for others, a strong sense of organization, and, within the context of all those things, a belief in the pursuit of happiness. Perhaps the most important principle underlying the Roman success story was, plainly and simply, the determination to succeed. If all roads lead to Rome, this is the one highway we must all take if we wish to be successful.

The Roman Secret of Success

How, then, do we attain success? As Aeneas's father, Anchises, told his son and all future Romans, we do it not by imitating others or trying to outdo them, but by discovering our own innate talents and actualizing them to the fullest. Anchises said:

> Let others make the bronze of statues breathe,
> as only *they* can do. Let *them* sculpt out of marble
> faces that live. Let *them* weave fancy words
> and picture the paths of planets and stars. Make it
> *your* business, Roman, to rule the world with the means
> that are yours: enforcing peace, sparing the humble,
> and crushing the proud in war.

True success, the Romans would be quick to tell us, does not come from copying others, but from being yourself. ·

A Mountain in Sinai

There are still other mountains we may choose to climb, and one of them, Mt. Horeb, is located in the Near Eastern wilderness of Sinai.

As you were reading the legends of Rome, you may have been struck by their similarity to stories found in the Old Testament. Romulus's murder of his brother Remus, for example, reminds us of Cain's murder of Abel. In the same way, the story of the twins being set adrift in a river and found by a benevolent stranger is reminiscent of the story of the infant Moses, who, like Romulus, was adopted and grew up to become a leader of his people. And just as Aeneas led his band of Trojan refugees westward across the Mediterranean in search of a promised land, so did Moses lead the Israelites out of Egyptian bondage eastward to a God-given homeland.

Before Moses became his people's savior, however, he lived in exile in the land of Midian. One day, when he was shepherding his flock, he saw a burning bush on Mt. Horeb and, climbing that mountain, found that the bush was not consumed by the fire. Just then the voice of God came from the burning bush, telling him he must return to Egypt in order to lead his people from slavery to freedom.

This dramatic story embodies a spiritual principle central to Judaism. The principle states that we are, in fact, the very thing Cain denied, our brother's keeper, and that we cannot stand idly by while others suffer. It is an ethical, and even an existential, principle Ulysses would readily understand as he sat on the beach of Calypso's island, thinking about the family that needed him, longing to return home. But in the development of the Jewish faith, this factor was exponentially raised to become an uncompromising demand for social justice. Centuries after Moses, we hear it in the impassioned cries of Jewish prophets like Isaiah and Amos, who sought to rouse the conscience of their countrymen and end the oppression of the weak. It is still the same voice from the burning bush, calling out our name today and requiring us to say, as did Moses, "Here I am." Without this moral imperative of conscience and action, even the Ten Commandments of Mt. Sinai would ring hollow. In its transcendent demand for universal social justice, Judaism went beyond the more limited aims of ancient Greece and Rome. In building our own personal temple, the pillar of justice is one we must add.

A Hill in Galilee

In the land of Israel there is another mount, where a sermon was given almost two thousand years ago. As Jesus traveled through Galilee, teaching and preaching, a multitude of people followed him. Seeing the crowd, he ascended the slopes of a hill beside the Sea of Galilee, gathered his disciples around him, and delivered what has come to be called the Sermon on the Mount.

Two accounts of his words exist, one in the Gospel According to Matthew, the other in the Gospel According to Luke. Neither Matthew nor Luke were present when Jesus spoke, and their accounts differ in many respects, but both versions agree that, to Jesus, personal religion could not be "business as usual." Instead, God demands that we go well beyond the letter of the law, even to the point of loving our enemies and doing good to those who hate us. It is this advanced degree of piety that God requires us to practice even though it flies in the face of popular wisdom. Significantly, using logic, the philosopher Socrates took a similar position some four centuries earlier.

The text of Jesus' sermon ends on the same note in both Matthew and Luke: a parable, or story with a moral, about two houses. One house, Jesus says, was built on rock, and withstood the pounding of rain and wind. The other house was built on sand, and was washed away. Whoever hears his message and ignores it, says Jesus, will be like the man who built his house on a foundation of sand.

In building *our* house, we must always look first to the foundation, building it with a pure heart.

Man-Made Mountains

The spiritual mountains we have climbed so far are works of nature, but there are others that are man-made. Natural mountains can inspire human beings with awe, but man-made mountains would not have existed had the human spirit not willed them to be.

The most ancient of these artificial mountains still stand in Egypt and Iraq, witnesses to the world's oldest civilizations. They have endured for more than four thousand years. Should alien archaeologists from a distant galaxy visit our planet someday and find it devoid of all human life, these monuments will constitute humanity's last will and testament, our race's final message to the cosmos. As we will see, it is a message written not only in matter, but also in myth. Together, they tell a story of humanity's longing for life after death.

So now let us begin our final odyssey, one that will take us farther back into time than we have already traveled, to a time before the heroic age of Greece and the founding of Rome, to a day before the bush burned in the desert and the sermon was delivered on the mount.

Ancient Egypt

There is an eternal bond between Egypt and the sun. Its radiance never fails to shine. In the red desert its heat can kill, but in the black earth of the river's banks it summons life.

Though the sun itself dies each day as it sinks below the western horizon, it is reborn at daybreak in the east. Thus the sun never truly dies, but only hides, waiting to return, waiting to bestow its life-giving energy on a waiting world.

From the sun's death and rebirth arose the Egyptians' faith in eternal life. What was true of the sun, they concluded, must also be true for humanity. It was the west that the people identified with death, and so put their cemeteries in the western desert where nothing but the spirit could grow. And it was the east, where the sun is reborn, that they identified with life.

The Egyptians called the divine sun Ra, and for ages the ruler of the land, the pharaoh, was thought of as his son. For this reason, the pyramids were called "stairways to heaven," because the spirit of the dead king was believed to ascend their slope to the sky to join his heavenly father.

Greek storytellers said that the sun was drawn across the sky by an invisible chariot driven by Helios, but the Egyptians said (and would you imagine anything else of a river folk?) that he was transported on a boat like those that ply the Nile.

The pious Egyptians, in fact, claimed that the sun was pushed across the sky by a huge invisible desert beetle. The insect was called the crab, or scarab, beetle because its pincers resemble those of a crab (called *scarabaeus* in Latin). The female beetle lays its eggs in a tiny ball of excrement (therefore some unceremoniously call her the dung beetle), excrement from which her young draw their first nourishment when they hatch. Marveling at the fact that new life emerged from the lifeless manure, the Egyptians called it a miracle. And so when they saw the orb of the sun traverse the sky, in their mind's eye they beheld an invisible beetle pushing the life-giving ball on its way. They also made imitation beetles from clay that they hung from strands on their necks in the belief that such amulets would grant them longer life. They also told how, at the beginning of time, the sun first rose from the petals of a lotus flower floating on the primordial sea.

As benevolent and life-giving as Ra was, Egypt would have been sheer desert had it not been for the river Nile. The Nile comes from the south and flows to the north until it empties into the sea. Thus to travel down the Nile you have only to yield to its currents, and it will take you to the sea.

But what if you should wish to return to the place from which you had come? In Egypt the wind blows from the north. Lift your sail then, the wind will carry you back to your beginnings. It seems the river wants us to travel, because it promises us a safe return.

If only life was a river. If only life could renew itself each year, certain as the rising of the stars. If only life could comfort us with the offered embrace of safe return for every journey taken.

Each year, as the star Sirius rose above the horizon just before dawn, the waters of the Nile began to rise as well. Eventually, as the days passed, the waters spilled over their banks, pouring over the peasants' fields. Before long, the lands were completely flooded. But the flood was not unexpected or sudden. Priestly astronomers had watched for the celestial signs of its coming, and the farmers had waited in their fields.

It is not destruction the waters brought. They carried with them rich silt from the headwaters of the river. And as the waters withdrew, slowly as they had come, they left behind their cargo of fertility on the peasants' fields, renewing and enriching the earth for future crops.

Were it not for the Nile's waters and the silt it bore, Egypt could not have supported human life. As Herodotus wrote in his *History*, "Egypt was the gift of the Nile."

Like the life-giving sun whose setting and rising could be counted upon, the ancient river was benevolent and dependable. It was also looked upon as a god, the god Hapi.

Life in Greece was never easy for farmers, but life in Egypt was sweet thanks to the gifts of the sun and the river. Each divinity showed its love to the Egyptian people in its own way, and they returned that love with worship and thanksgiving.

The vegetative life that grew in Egypt's soil had its own god. Osiris was the god of fertility, and to represent that fact artists painted the skin of his effigies green so he would resemble the growing plants he animated.

His power was like the power of Greek Demeter, but, unlike her, he did not lose his daughter to the god of death. Instead, he lost his own life and *became* the god of death. Therefore he was Demeter and Hades combined—a curious combination that joined fertility and death in one deity. But, more than that, he held out to those who died the promise of eternal life. His story was perhaps the strangest the Egyptians told, and the easiest to accept.

The Legend of Osiris

To begin to understand this tale you must understand that no Egyptian would have wanted to stop living. To live forever in happiness would have been their dream. And it was a dream sustained by the world they lived in, a world in which so little changed that the very thought of a thing ending seldom entered their minds. The sun-god Ra and the river-god Hapi testified to the everlasting and unchanging, to a future mirrored in the past. Indeed, in the Egyptian language the word for life, *ankh*, was the same as for mirror. The life to come was the reflection of the life that had been, just as ages to come would always reflect ages past.

In the beginning, Osiris was a mortal king and a good and decent man. He was beloved by his wife and honored by his people. But he was hated by his jealous brother Seth. Seth, in fact, was so jealous, he plotted to murder his brother.

On Osiris's birthday, Seth arranged a party with special entertainment: a magic show in which he, Seth, would be the magician. "I need a volunteer to climb into this box," he announced, and Osiris willingly volunteered. Seth's servants then swiftly nailed the lid shut and carried the box from the palace. Then, to the horror of the guests, Seth ordered it thrown into the sea so Osiris would die.

Osiris did die, and the waves carried the box over the sea for many days until it reached the shores of Phoenicia. A grieving Isis, Osiris's loving wife, searched far and wide for the coffin, finally found it, and brought the corpse back to Egypt for burial.

But Seth's vengeance was not sated. He hacked the corpse into fourteen pieces and scattered them up and down the valley of the Nile so Osiris could not be given a proper burial. Isis searched for these too and found them all except for one, the penis, which a Nile fish had eaten. According to one version, Isis buried each part of her husband's mutilated body wherever she found it, and in time a commemorative shrine was built over the spot where each piece was interred. (This is why there were so many shrines to Osiris along the Nile.) Or, according to another more popular version, Isis gathered the parts together and brought them back to the royal palace where she laid them out on a funerary bed.

As she knelt beside the mutilated corpse and wept, the god Anubis appeared. Anubis was the god of cemeteries and funerals, jackal-headed because jackals were wont to prowl Egypt's cemeteries. Anubis took pity on Isis and wrapped the pieces of Osiris's body in layer after layer of linen bandages until they collectively resembled the corpse that Osiris had formerly been. Anubis even attached an artificial penis to make up for the one that had been lost. Then he recited a litany of magical spells and incantations and suddenly the corpse sat up! Osiris had been brought back to life.

Thereafter Osiris became the king of the dead, but a death that was really life. Like Jesus, he promised to all those who would live a good and morally pure life a continuation of that existence in a kingdom of heaven with everlasting happiness and contentment. Isis became Osiris's loving queen. And, with the help of the artificial penis Anubis had provided, they even had a child, a son, hawk-headed Horus, who one day, when he was a man, fought Seth and defeated him in a mighty battle to avenge the wrong done to his father.

Unlike Hades and Persephone, who ruled over a dark, dismal, and disembodied kingdom where no pleasure was possible and everything was insubstantial, Osiris and Isis reigned over a happy realm in which those who had died on Earth, mummified as Osiris had been, lived on in an eternal bliss of sensual pleasure, enjoying all the pursuits and possessions they enjoyed on Earth and sharing the company of those they loved.

Perhaps only a land like Egypt, so blessed by the gods of nature, could have created an afterlife so rich in promise. The somber Greek view of the afterlife may have made the Greeks live all the more intensely because they knew this was the only life they would ever have. But that very realism denied them the comforting hope the Egyptians enjoyed. Perhaps that is why so many Greeks who settled in Egypt and learned its ways chose to be buried in the Egyptian style, wrapped like Osiris, in the hope that he and Isis would look kindly after their souls and would permit them to be immigrants to a joyous hereafter.

The Journey of the Soul

The ancient Egyptians believed that the body was the dwelling place of the spirit, which is why they preserved it. As for the spirit itself, it came in three forms: the *ka*, the *ba*, and the *akh*. The *ka* was the closest to what the Greeks would have called a ghost, the sort that dwelt in Hades's realm. The *ka* was the spiritual double of the person, and it journeyed to the kingdom of Osiris to live there forever. At the same time, however, it could accept nourishment from offerings left at the tomb by its loved ones. The *ba* was the soul conceived in the form of a human-headed bird that, during the day, could fly invisibly to the places it had known during its lifetime and lovingly watch over those it knew. As for the *akh*, it dwelt serenely among the stars, forever circling the North Star in heaven.

No soul, however, was automatically guaranteed a life of everlasting happiness. The soul, or *ka*, had to first make a dangerous journey from the east following the path of the sun and then travel into the darkness of the netherworld that lies beneath the sun's setting place in the west. In the darkness the soul would encounter monsters as fearsome as any Hercules or Perseus ever met, and obstacles as daunting as any faced by Ulysses on his odyssey. Aiding the soul, however, was a guidebook, a scroll placed in the tomb that detailed the prayers and hymns, the spells and incantations by which both monsters and obstacles could be overcome. Whoever could afford such a scroll would have it prepared by a scribe long before the day of their death. Today, we collectively call these scrolls the *Book of the Dead*.

Upon reaching the kingdom of Osiris, the soul was interrogated by none other than the god of wisdom himself, ibis-headed Thoth. But the questions Thoth asked were always the same and the answers were predictable, based as they were upon tradition. Besides, they were all conveniently listed for easy reference in the *Book of the Dead*.

Next followed a confession before a tribunal of forty-two gods, to each of whom a separate confession of good conduct was made.

Lastly came the greatest test of all, for which no purchased scroll could prepare the soul, no memorized answers suffice. The heart was placed on a scale, and against it was balanced the ostrich feather of truth. If the heart was as light as the feather, the pan of the scale would not dip, and a blessed immortality for the soul was assured. But if the heart was heavy with sin, its pan would sink, and instantly the soul would be swallowed by the waiting Devourer, the hideous beast Amam. Then the deceased would die for a second time, but this time forever.

For those who passed the final test there was a life of eternal bliss and endless sensual pleasure: music to delight the ear, dancing to charm the eye, the savor of food and the scent of wine, and nearby the touch of one's beloved.

It is to this end that the Egyptians worked so long and hard preparing for the afterlife. Compared to the brevity of this life, its delights were endless and made the effort worthwhile. The Egyptians were not obsessed with death. Rather they loved life and could not bear the thought of losing it.

The simple peasant would live a simple peasant's life, but without hardship or suffering, hunger or thirst. The nobleman would live the nobleman's life, enjoying the bounty of his estate and laboring honorably in the service of his king. Thus the same order of society would exist in the hereafter even as it had existed among the living.

The Pyramids and the Sphinx

A hundred miles south of Alexandria stands the Great Pyramid of Pharaoh Cheops. It may be the oldest monument in the world. So powerful was this king that hundreds of thousands labored to build his tomb. Even in its silence the tomb teaches many lessons.

It teaches that what we build persists long after we die. At least, that is true for kings who can command the labor of thousands to rear up monuments to their glory. For the workers themselves little can be said except that they piously labored to serve their master. His is the memory they served; their own is almost entirely lost.

The Great Pyramid testifies to massive egotism, the egotism of the mighty. But it also testifies to the emptiness of their dreams. Greed has crushed mighty Cheops's hopes. Others, not he, claimed his treasure.

Stolen, the gold was melted down long ago. The hieroglyphs that bore his name dissolved in the boiling cauldron of grave-robbing thieves. Thus his pyramid teaches us both the bigness and the smallness of man who seeks to live through his possessions.

Not far from the Great Pyramid, the Sphinx sprawls on the desert floor. It is a great lion carved from the limestone bedrock. Much of it is often covered in deep and drifting sand. The face of the Sphinx is believed to be the face of a pharaoh who ruled Egypt many centuries ago. The ancients called him Khaf-re, or Chephren, the successor of Cheops. Beside the Sphinx is the stone causeway that leads from the River Nile to Khaf-re's pyramid. The Sphinx guards the way.

He seems a proud beast, if beast we should call him. His face is turned toward the sun that rises from the eastern desert. Each morning his eyes behold the sunrise. The Sphinx has already seen a million and a half sunrises. Yet I wonder if he was not blinded long ago by all that light. There is, after all, only so much burning light the eyes can behold before they cease to see. And all the more true for the Great Sphinx, who was condemned by art never to blink. Yet I suspect he must know the sun when it rises by its warmth as it gently touches, soft ray upon soft ray, the stone of his face, chilled by the cold of the long, blue desert night. They do not speak, the sun and the Sphinx, but they know each other all the same.

This Sphinx is very proud and not at all frightening, but visitors *were* frightened by him long ago. They were Greeks, who most assuredly should not have been frightened by what can be understood, least of all a work of art that only *resembles* a living thing, but is not itself living. These Greeks may have been soldiers, mercenaries who came from Greece to serve a foreign king. As soldiers then, and not philosophers, and from a time before the Greeks had made stone statues of their own, they would have been rightly frightened by a beast so big, thought it a monster, and regarded it with awe. Perhaps that is why in Greek tradition the Sphinx became a monster that terrified man, like the one Oedipus met on the road to Thebes.

When Herodotus visited Egypt in the fifth century, he was told of a strange and sacred bird (he admits he never saw it himself), a bird called the phoenix. Ornate with red and gold plumage, it came to Egypt every five hundred years, bearing the embalmed corpse of its father in a huge resinous egg, which the bird dutifully deposited in the temple of Ra.

Others disputed Herodotus and claimed the phoenix was a stranger bird still, that it was in fact its own parent. When it sensed it was about to die, it built a great pyre and climbed upon it. And when the pyre was ignited and the body of the old phoenix was burnt, out of its ashes rose a new bird. Thus the phoenix was resurrected out of the ruins of itself, and was eternally renewed.

Indeed, ancient Egypt is itself the phoenix. From its quest for eternal life it attained what it sought. Its enduring monuments made it eternal.

Ancient Mesopotamia

Mesopotamia is the name historians give to ancient Iraq. The name means "the land between the rivers," and the rivers are the Tigris (to the east) and the Euphrates (to the west). Along their fertile banks and nourished by their waters, an early civilization flourished around the same time that civilization began in Egypt. It was the aquatic environment in both countries and the agricultural abundance it nurtured that enabled the world's first civilizations to arise in these lands.

But the Tigris and Euphrates were very different from the Nile. The waters of the Nile rose gently and with predictable regularity every year, gradually overflowing the river's banks and depositing fresh, fertilizing silt over the farmers' fields. The Tigris and Euphrates flooded also, but violently and unpredictably, washing away the works of man and destroying whole cities.

The striking ecological differences between Egypt and Mesopotamia generated dramatically different ideologies. While the ancient Egyptians felt gratitude for the benevolence of the gods, the ancient Mesopotamians feared their capricious rage. While the Egyptians optimistically believed in the certainty of immortality, the Mesopotamians pessimistically concluded that there was little beyond this life that man could hope for.

In humble recognition of their own impotence in controlling their fate, the Mesopotamians raised up shrines to the gods, mounting them on lofty stepped platforms called *ziggurats*. In the flat, alluvial plain in which they lived, the ziggurats served as artificial mountains that allowed the gods to descend more readily from heaven to the earth.

Mesopotamia, however, was not blessed with stone as was Egypt. Therefore the Mesopotamians constructed their stepped pyramids out of brick made from the mud and clay of their rivers. Because of this fact, their monuments have not lasted like those of Egypt. Even so, their crumbling profiles still dot the now-arid landscape of Iraq, like old scoops of chocolate ice cream melting beneath the blazing sun.

Deprived of a theology of hope, the people of Mesopotamia nevertheless clung to the slender belief that something might lie beyond the grave. We know this from the offerings reverentially placed in graves beside the bodies of the dead by their relatives so that their loved ones could enjoy an afterlife of comfort. Some royal graves, such as those unearthed at the city of Ur, even contained splendid golden armor and jewelry befitting their occupants, as well as lyres and game boards to amuse them during the endless hours of eternity. But most people did not anticipate such spiritual luxury or ease. Instead, the netherworld was portrayed in dark and somber tones like Homer's Hades. And, like Hades, it was the depressing destination that was everybody's "end of the line." But unlike the ancient Greeks, the people of ancient Mesopotamia were not inspired, in the face of death, to live their lives with passionate and defiant intensity.

The Legend of Gilgamesh

Of all the works of Mesopotamian literature, the most powerful is *The Epic of Gilgamesh*. The epic is named for its central character, Gilgamesh, a hero-king who searched for the secret of eternal life and, after great effort, ultimately found wisdom and its consolation.

Early in his reign over the city of Uruk, Gilgamesh exercised his power arrogantly, harassing young men and sleeping with their intended brides before they were wed. To end his reign of oppression, the gods created a champion named Enkidu, a hairy, muscular brute who lived in the wild and, like Tarzan, called the animals his friends. Eventually, Enkidu and Gilgamesh clashed with each other and wrestled to a draw. Thereafter they became buddies, and joined together in a great adventure: to slay the monster Humbaba who guarded the Cedar Forest. Though they were successful, a later incident cost Enkidu his life. Insane with grief over the death of his best friend, and awakened to the fact of his own mortality, Gilgamesh went on a quest to obtain the secret of eternal life. He could learn it if he found a wise man named Utnapishtim, who, like Noah, had survived the Great Flood.

In the course of his long and dangerous journey, Gilgamesh stopped at a tavern tended by a divine barmaid. Once she learned of his mission, she pointed out its futility, and urged Gilgamesh to desist.

> The life you're looking for
> you'll never find,
> for when the gods made man
> death is what they saved for him,
> reserving life for themselves.
> So, Gilgamesh, eat and drink your fill.
> Celebrate day and night,
> and make every day a festival.
> Night and day dance and play.
> Make sure your clothes are sparkling;
> rinse your hair and bathe.
> Mind the child that holds your hand,
> and let your wife enjoy your embrace.
> For *this* is the proper business of man.

Undissuaded however, Gilgamesh continued on his quest, crossing the Waters of Death to the place where Utnapishtim dwelled. Utnapishtim had compassion for the weary traveler and told him about a magic plant that grew at the bottom of the sea, a plant that could restore a person's youth. After diving and plucking the plant from the sea floor, Gilgamesh started on his homeward way. Stopping beside a pool to rest, he set the plant down at the water's edge, only to have a serpent steal it away. Thus he lost his last hope of gaining eternal life.

Heartbroken, Gilgamesh returned to his city. As he approached it, he gazed upon its mighty walls, walls that he himself had built. Only then did he realize that our true salvation lies not in a vain quest for immortality, but rather in the works we leave behind. Our true mission is to live for the present and love those who love us, blessing others by our acts.

Two Lands; Two Ways

The Tigris and Euphrates flowed from north to south, the Nile from south to north. Similarly, the people of the two lands viewed death from different perspectives: the Mesopotamians believing in life's grim finality, the Egyptians in its joyous continuation. Yet each people found consolation from its search, and spiritual direction from its guiding myths.

Other Mountains

East of Egypt and Mesopotamia are other mountains to climb, the mountains that symbolize the wisdom of Asia. Such a journey exceeds the limits of this short work, but there are other guidebooks to take you the rest of the way.

Because our main theme has been Greek wisdom, perhaps it would be fitting to close with another Hellenic myth.

The Story of Orion

The hunter Orion had long pursued the princess Merope and wanted to marry her. But her father kept putting Orion off. At last, Orion could not stand the frustration, and he raped Merope. In vengeance, her father blinded Orion while he slept.

Later, Orion learned that his sight could be restored, and his sin cleansed, if he traveled to the east and turned his eyes toward the sun as it rose from the ocean at the edge of the world. But how could Orion make such a long journey if he was blind?

According to the myth, he found a young boy to guide him. Hoisting the boy on his shoulders, Orion headed east 'til they came to the edge of the world where the dawn began. As the sun started to rise, Orion turned his eyes toward its warming rays, and was cured of the blindness that had afflicted his body and soul. Eventually when Orion died, he was placed among the stars to serve as a constellation and everlasting guide for mankind.

Shining in the celestial darkness, the hunter Orion declares that with help each of us, whatever our sins, can make a long journey as he did. And at the end of that journey, our blindness can be cured by the blazing light of a distant sun. That sun, the light of wisdom, waits for us even now.

EPILOGUE

REACHING THE SUMMIT

In emulating the ancient Greeks and symbolically climbing Olympus, we must recognize that those who preceded us never attained the summit. The ancient Greeks were humans like ourselves, filled with imperfections. But, also like ourselves, they also aspired to become something better than they were. It is that determined effort that inspires us today.

In fact, there *is* no summit, no final point that will mark the end of our struggles. Even if there were, life would be too short for us to reach it. Instead, climbing Olympus means to climb on. It is the continual process of becoming—rather than the fact of having become—that must be our aim.

The ancient Greeks do not offer final answers. That is not their legacy to us. Their gift is the gift of enduring questions: What does it mean to be human? What *can* it mean? What do we owe ourselves? What do we owe to others? What are the limits to which we can go? What is the price we must pay to get there?

These questions defy the borders of space and time, of nationality and history. The classical tradition has lived on for more than two millennia because each successive generation heard these questions speak directly to it, and found in classical literature a pertinent commentary on its own times. That is true because the classical tradition is rooted in the quest to understand human nature and is therefore universal.

Should aliens someday land on our planet, they will need to go no farther than the myths of Greece to understand our race. And if that day
should come, we will need to hand them no other book. Until then, Mt.
Olympus still stands, snow-capped and proud, urging us on to *become*.

If you have built castles in the air,
your work need not be lost;
that is where they should be.
Now put the foundations under them.

—Henry David Thoreau, *Walden*

Major Gods of Greece

The Olympian Gods*

The names in parentheses are those given to these gods by the Romans.

Zeus (Jupiter): king of the gods, god of justice

Hera (Juno): queen of the gods, sister and wife of Zeus

Poseidon (Neptune): god of the sea, brother of Zeus

Demeter (Ceres): goddess of grain and earthly fertility, sister of Zeus

Hestia (Vesta): goddess of the hearth and home, sister of Zeus

Zeus's Sons

Ares (Mars): god of war

Apollo (Apollo): god of light, prophecy, music, poetry, and dance

Hermes (Mercury): messenger of the gods, god of commerce

Hephaestus (Vulcan): the craftsman god

Zeus's Daughters

Athena (Minerva): virgin goddess of wisdom and intelligence, protectress of Athens

Artemis (Diana): virgin goddess of hunting, twin sister of Apollo

Aphrodite (Venus): goddess of sexual attraction and passion (according to another myth, born of the god Uranus)

Other Deities

Hades (Pluto): god of the dead, brother of Zeus

Dionysus (Bacchus): god of wine (eventually took Hestia's place among the twelve Olympians)

Heracles (Hercules): great hero who, upon his death, became the thirteenth Olympian

Major Events in Ancient Greek History

About 1900 B.C.   The first Greek-speaking immigrants set-
                               tle in the land we call Greece.

About 1700 B.C.   The city of Mycenae begins its rise to
                               prominence.

About 1450 B.C.   The Mycenaeans seize control of Knossos.

About 1270–1260 B.C.   The Trojan War (Greeks vs. Trojans)

About 1200–1100 B.C.   The collapse of the Mycenaean Empire

About 1100–750 B.C.   The Dark Ages

About 750–490 B.C.   The Archaic Period

About 490–404 B.C.   The Classical Period

   The Persian Wars   (Greeks vs. Persians: 490 & 480–479 B.C.)

   The Peloponnesian War   (Athens vs. Sparta: 431–404 B.C.)

336–323 B.C.   The career of Alexander the Great and the
                               beginning of the Hellenistic Age

146 B.C.   Rome gains dominance over Greece.

Glossary of Ancient Names

Abel: Son of Adam and Eve, brother of Cain

Achilles: Warrior and central character in Homer's *The Iliad*

Acropolis: Rocky hill in central Athens; site of the Parthenon and other temples to Athena

Admetus: Self-centered husband of Alcestis

Aeacus: An ancestor of Achilles

Aeëtes: Keeper of the Golden Fleece

Aegeus: King of Athens, father of Theseus

Aeneas: Trojan prince and hero of Vergil's *Aeneid*

Aeneid: National epic of Rome; composed by the poet Vergil

Aeolus: Keeper of the winds

Aeschylus: Athenian playwright specializing in tragedies including *Agamemnon* and *Prometheus Bound*

Aesclepius: God of healing

Agamemnon: King of Mycenae and commander-in-chief of the Greek army at Troy

Ajax: Greek warrior who fought at Troy

Alba Longa: Town in Italy where Romulus and Remus were born

Alcestis: Self-sacrificing wife of King Admetus

Alcmene: Mother of Hercules

Alexander the Great: Charismatic Macedonian general and king

Alexandria: Egyptian city founded by Alexander the Great

Amam: A monster who devoured sinful souls in the Egyptian netherworld

Amos: Hebrew prophet

Amun: Egyptian god whose oracle was visited by Alexander the Great

Anchises: Father of the Trojan hero Aeneas

Antigone: Daughter of Oedipus

Anubis: Egyptian god of funerals and cemeteries

Aphrodite: Greek goddess of love

Apollo: Greek and Roman god of light and prophecy

Arachne: Prideful weaver transformed into a spider by Athena

Ares: Greek god of war

Argo: Boat used by Jason and the Argonauts to search for the Golden Fleece

Argonauts: Heroes who sailed with Jason on the Argo

Argus: Designer of the Argo; also the name of a hundred-eyed guard as well as Ulysses's faithful dog

Ariadne: Cretan princess who fell in love with Theseus

Aristophanes: Athenian playwright specializing in comedies, including *The Clouds* and *Lysistrata*

Aristotle: Greek philosopher, student of Plato, and tutor of Alexander the Great

Artemis: Greek goddess of hunting, sister of Apollo

Atalanta: Fleet runner who challenged each suitor to a race

Atlantis: Legendary civilization that sank beneath the sea

Athena: Greek goddess of wisdom and intelligence

Athens: Birthplace of Greece's Golden Age

Augean Stables: Royal stables cleaned by Hercules

Bacchus: Greek and Roman god of wine

Baucis: Aged wife of Philemon

Bacchae: Female devotees of the god of wine; known for their orgiastic rites

Bucephalia: City named after Alexander the Great's horse

Bucephalus: Faithful horse of Alexander the Great

Cadmus: Dragon-slayer and bringer of the alphabet to Greece

Cain: Murderous brother of Abel

Calchas: Greek seer during the days of the Trojan War

Callicrates: Classical architect and codesigner of the Parthenon

Calydonian Boar: Beast hunted down by the hero Meleager

Calypso: Divine temptress who tried to detain Ulysses

Caryae: City in Greece and hometown of the Caryatids

Caryatids: Enslaved women of Caryae; immortalized in sculpture as supporting columns of the Erechtheum

Cassandra: Cursed by Apollo with a gift of prophecy no one would believe

Cattle of Geryon: A herd rustled by Hercules

Centaurs: Barbaric creatures, half-human and half-horse

Cerberus: Watchdog who guarded the entry to the land of the dead

Ceres: Roman goddess of grain

Ceryneian Deer: Animal hunted by Hercules

Charon: Ferryman of the dead

Charybdis: Whirlpool that almost swallowed Ulysses

Cheops: Egyptian pharaoh and builder of the Great Pyramid

Chephren: Egyptian pharaoh thought to be portrayed by the Sphinx

Chiron: A benevolent Centaur, tutor of Achilles

Chronos: The Greek word for "time"

Clymene: Mother of Phaëthon

Clytaemnestra: Vengeful wife of King Agamemnon

Cocalus: Sicilian king who offered Daedalus asylum

Colchis: Land of the Golden Fleece

Colosseum: Gladiatorial amphitheater in Rome

Corinth: Greek city and adoptive hometown of Oedipus

Creon: Uncle of Antigone

Croesus: Fabulously wealthy Lydian king

Cyclops: One-eyed giant and enemy of Ulysses

Cyprus: Island home of Pygmalion

Cythera: Greek island that welcomed newly born Aphrodite

Daedalus: Cretan inventor and designer of the Labyrinth

Delphi: Home of the god Apollo and his prophetic priestess

Demeter: Greek goddess of grain

Deucalion: The Greek "Noah"

Diana: Roman goddess of hunting, sister to Apollo

Dido: North African queen who fell in love with Aeneas

Diogenes: Anti-materialistic Greek philosopher

Diomedes: Owner of man-eating horses sought by Hercules; also the name of a Greek warrior who fought at Troy

Dionysus: Greek god of wine and patron god of theater (synonymous with Bacchus)

Echo: Nymph who fell in love with Narcissus

Eidothea: Daughter of the Old Man of the Sea

Enkidu: Rough-hewn friend of the Mesopotamian hero Gilgamesh

Eos: Goddess of the dawn, loved Tithonus

Erechtheum: Temple on the Acropolis featuring the Caryatids

Eris: Goddess of trouble

Eros: Son of Aphrodite and youthful god of love

Erymanthian Boar: Quarry sought by Hercules as one of his Labors

Euphrates: Mesopotamian river

Euripides: Athenian dramatist, author of tragedies including *Hippolytus, Medea, The Bacchae,* and *Alcestis*

Europa: Phoenician princess kidnapped by Zeus

Eurydice: Orpheus's beloved, whom he sought to retrieve from the kingdom of Hades

Eurystheus: King who commanded Hercules to perform Twelve Labors

Fates: Three goddesses who jointly determined the destinies of humans

Gaea: Primal goddess of the earth

Galatea: Statue carved by Pygmalion and brought to life by Aphrodite

Gilgamesh: Mesopotamian epic hero

Glaucus: Warrior who fought on the side of Troy in the Trojan War

Gordion: Home of the Gordion Knot severed by Alexander the Great

Gyges: Possessor of a ring that endowed the wearer with invisibility

Hades: Divine king of the land of the dead

Hapi: Egyptian god of the Nile

Hector: Trojan hero described in *The Iliad*

Helen: Wife of King Menelaus of Sparta; abandoned her husband and sailed to Troy with her lover Paris, igniting the Trojan War

Helios: God of the sun and father of Phaëthon

Hephaestus: God of craftsmanship

Hera: Queen of the Greek gods and wife to Zeus

Heracles: An alternate spelling of "Hercules"

Heraclitus: Greek philosopher who spoke of the constant change in life

Hercules: Muscular hero and son of Zeus and Alcmene

Hermes: Greek messenger god

Herodotus: Greek historian renowned as "the father of history"

Hesiod: Greek epic poet; one of the earliest literary sources for Greek myth

Hesperides: Goddesses who guarded golden apples sought by Hercules in one of his Labors

Hestia: Greek goddess of the hearth

Hippolyta: Queen of the warlike Amazons

Hippolytus: Son of Theseus and object of Phaedra's desire

Hippomenes: Suitor of Atalanta, defeated her in a footrace with the help of golden apples

Homer: Revered as Greece's greatest poet, author of *The Iliad* and *The Odyssey*

Horus: Egyptian god, son of Osiris and Isis

Humbaba: Mesopotamian monster defeated by Gilgamesh and Enkidu

Hydra: Multi-headed water monster slain by Hercules

Icarus: Son of Daedalus, first fatality in aviation history

Ictinus: Codesigner of the Parthenon, with Callicrates

Iliad: Homeric poem describing the effects of Achilles's wrath during the Trojan War

Iphigenia: Daughter of Agamemnon, ritually sacrificed by her father

Isaiah: Hebrew prophet

Isis: Egyptian goddess and wife of Osiris

Ithaca: Island home of the hero Ulysses

Janus: Two-faced Roman god of beginnings; origin of the month "January"

Jason: Hero who searched for the Golden Fleece with Medea's help

Jesus: Central figure of the Christian faith and the New Testament

Juno: Queen of the Roman gods and wife of Jupiter

Jupiter: King of the Roman gods (equivalent to Zeus)

Knossos: City on the island on Crete; site of the palace of King Minos

Kronos: Divine son of Uranus and father of Zeus

Labyrinth: Maze designed by Daedalus

Laertes: Father of Ulysses

Laocoön: Trojan priest who was suspicious of the Trojan Horse

Lapiths: Greek tribesmen who fought the Centaurs

Leto: Mother of the gods Apollo and Artemis

Livy: Roman historian

Lotus-Eaters: Friendly addicts encountered by Ulysses and his men

Luke: Author of one of the Four Gospels of the New Testament

Maenads: Female devotees of Dionysus

Marathon: Site of a Greek victory over the Persians

Mars: Roman god of war

Matthew: Author of one of the Four Gospels of the New Testament

Medea: Sorceress who fell tragically in love with Jason

Medusa: A snaky-haired monster whose gaze could petrify those who looked into her eyes; slain by Perseus

Meleager: Heroic Greek hunter

Menelaus: King of Sparta and husband of Helen

Merope: A princess desired by Orion

Midas: King whose touch could turn everything to gold

Midian: Land in the Sinai Peninsula where Moses lived in exile

Mimnermus: Greek elegiac poet who wrote poems of mourning and love

Minerva: Roman goddess of wisdom

Minos: King of Crete, father of Ariadne, and builder of the Labyrinth

Minotaur: Cretan monster, half-man, half-bull

Moses: Liberated the Israelites, gave the Ten Commandments

Mt. Aetna: Volcanic mountain in Sicily beneath which monsters were buried

Mt. Horeb: Mountain in the Sinai Peninsula, site of the "Burning Bush"

Mt. Ida: Mountain near Troy, site of "The Judgment of Paris"

Mt. Olympus: Highest mountain in Greece and home of the Greek gods

Mt. Parnassus: Mountain overlooking Delphi and Apollo's temple

Mt. Sinai: Mountain in the Sinai Peninsula where the Ten Commandments were given

Mycenae: Most powerful city in Greece at the time of the Trojan War

Myron: Athenian sculptor famous for *The Discus Thrower*

Narcissus: Young man who fell in love with his own reflection

Nemean Lion: A beast killed by Hercules

Neptune: Roman god of the sea

Nile: Egypt's great river

Niobe: Prideful mother whose children were slain by the gods

Numitor: Benevolent grandfather of Romulus and Remus

Odysseus: Alternate name for Ulysses, hero of *The Odyssey*

Odyssey: Homer's epic story of the adventures of Ulysses (Odysseus)

Oedipus: King who killed his father and married his mother in fulfillment of a prophecy

Olympia: Home of the Olympic Games

Orion: Hunter who was blinded and later regained his sight

Orpheus: Renowned musician who loved Eurydice and sought to reclaim her from the kingdom of Hades

Osiris: Egyptian god of the dead

Ovid: Roman love poet and author of *The Metamorphoses*

Palatine Hill: One of the seven hills of Rome; site where a she-wolf nursed Romulus and Remus

Pandora: Archetypal woman created by the gods to bring woes to mankind

Paris: Trojan prince and lover of Helen

Parthenon: Sanctuary dedicated to Athena; the largest and most famous temple on Athens's Acropolis

Pasiphaë: Wife of King Minos of Crete; became enamored of a bull and gave birth to the Minotaur

Patroclus: Loyal comrade of Achilles

Peleus: Father of Achilles

Peloponnesian War: Fifth century B.C. war between Athens and Sparta

Penelope: Faithful wife of Ulysses

Pentheus: Legendary opponent of Dionysus

Pericles: Leading statesman of Athens during its Golden Age

Persepolis: Royal capital of the Persian Empire

Persephone: Daughter of the goddess Demeter, kidnapped by Hades

Perseus: Heroic slayer of Medusa and rescuer of Andromeda

Persian Wars: Fifth century B.C. wars between the Greeks and the ancient Iranians

Phaedra: Wife of Theseus; became enamored of her stepson Hippolytus

Phaëthon: Son of the sun-god Helios; died as a result of seeking the identity of his father

Pharos: Island north of the Nile delta and place where Menelaus was marooned

Pheidippides: Famous Greek runner; may have run the first Marathon race in history

Phidias: Athenian sculptor; designed the sculptural decoration of the Parthenon

Philemon: Aged husband of Baucis

Philip: Macedonian king and father of Alexander the Great

Phrygia: Kingdom located in ancient Turkey

Pindar: Greek poet who wrote odes praising victors

Pirithoüs: King of the Lapiths

Plato: Greek philosopher; student of Socrates and teacher of Aristotle; author of *The Republic*

Plotinus: Greek philosopher

Pluto: Roman god of the netherworld

Polycleitus: Athenian sculptor of the classical period

Polyphemus: Personal name of the Cyclops who trapped Ulysses

Poseidon: Greek god of the sea

Procrustes: Malevolent host who fitted his guests to a special bed

Prodicus: Friend of Socrates

Prometheus: Benefactor of mankind; punished by Zeus for stealing fire

Protagoras: Greek sophist and contemporary of Socrates

Proteus: The Old Man of the Sea; had the power to change his shape when threatened

Psyche: Young woman who fell tragically in love with Eros

Ptolemies: Rulers of Egypt following the death of Alexander the Great

Pygmalion: Man who fell in love with Galatea, a statue he had created

Pyramus: Tragic young lover of Thisbe

Pyrrha: Deucalion's wife

Pythagoras: Greek philosopher and mathematician

Python: Serpentine monster slain by Apollo

Ra: Egyptian god of the sun

Remus: Twin brother of Romulus

Rhea: Mother of Zeus and his siblings

Romulus: Twin brother of Remus and founder of Rome

Sabines: A tribe whose women were raped by Romulus and his men

Santorini: Modern name for the island of Thera

Sappho: Greek erotic poet

Scylla: Multiheaded monster encountered by Ulysses and his men on their homeward voyage

Semele: Lover of Zeus; incinerated by his radiance; gave birth to Dionysus

Seth: Egyptian god, brother and murderer of Osiris

Simonides: Greek poet who wrote about time

Sirens: Musical temptresses encountered by Ulysses and his men

Sisyphus: Man tortured in the underworld by the compulsion to push a boulder over a hill

Socrates: Greek philosopher executed for his questioning spirit; teacher of Plato

Solon: Athenian statesman and traveler

Sophocles: Athenian dramatist; author of tragedies including *Oedipus the King* and *Antigone*

Sparta: Hometown of Greece's most feared warriors

Sphinx: Riddling monster who challenged Oedipus; also, in Egyptian art, a man-headed lion

Stymphalian Birds: Death-dealing birds sought by Hercules in one of his Labors

Styx: River that flowed through the Greek netherworld

Symplagades: Clashing rocks that threatened Jason's ship

Tantalus: Man tortured by hunger and thirst in the kingdom of Hades

Telemachus: Son of Ulysses

Telesterion: Prime sanctuary of the Eleusinian Mysteries

Thebes: City that Oedipus came to rule

Theodosius: Christian emperor of Rome who terminated the Olympic Games and closed the temple of Apollo at Delphi

Thera: Volcanic island in the Aegean; its eruption may have inspired the legend of Atlantis

Thermopylae: Pass defended by three hundred Spartan warriors against assault by the Persian army

Theseus: Slayer of the Minotaur, father of Hippolytus and husband of Phaedra

Thessaly: Region in northern Greece

Thespis: The theater's first actor

Thetis: Sea-nymph and mother of Achilles

Thisbe: Young woman who took her own life because of her love for Pyramus

Thoth: Egyptian god of wisdom

Thucydides: Athenian general and historian who described the war between Athens and Sparta

Tiber: River that flows through Rome

Tigris: River that, with the Euphrates, defines the outlines of Mesopotamia

Tiresias: A blind prophet who appears in plays of Sophocles

Titans: Primal Greek deities who fought for supremacy against the gods of Olympus

Tithonus: Man condemned to perpetual aging because of an ill-considered wish

Tityus: Man tortured in the netherworld by a voracious vulture

Trojan Horse: A wooden horse secretly filled with Greek commandos intent on Troy's capture

Troy: Site of the famous Trojan War; located on the northwest coast of present-day Turkey; excavated by Heinrich Schliemann

Ulysses: Hero of Homer's *The Odyssey*, alternately called Odysseus

Ur: Mesopotamian city

Uranus: Primal Greek god of the sky, castrated by his son Kronos

Uruk: Mesopotamian city and hometown of Gilgamesh

Utnapishtim: Noah-like survivor of the Babylonian Flood, visited by Gilgamesh

Venus: Roman goddess of love

Vergil: Roman poet and author of *The Aeneid*

Vesta: Roman goddess of the hearth

Vulcan: Roman blacksmith god

Wooden Horse: A horse built by the Greeks out of wood to help them capture Troy; also known as the Trojan Horse

Zeus: King of the Greek gods

FURTHER READING

Original Sources

The most direct access to the ancient Greek mind is through their literature and art, but because their art rarely comes with captions, it is to their literature that we must turn for the most explicit articulation of their ideas.

The ancient Greek language continues to be taught at many good universities, and we are fortunate also to possess modern translations of all the major classical authors, with new translations being published every year. Listed below are some of the most outstanding Greek writers along with the subjects they wrote on.

Epic: Homer, Hesiod, and Apollonius Rhodius
Lyric Poetry: Sappho, Pindar
Drama: Aeschylus, Sophocles, and Euripides (for tragedy)
     Aristophanes and Menander (for comedy)
History: Herodotus and Thucydides
Philosophy: Plato and Aristotle
Biography: Plutarch

My best advice for the beginner is to go to a very good bookstore or library and sample the available translations of the authors or works you are most intrigued by. When you find a translation that is clear and seems to speak directly to you, that is the one to choose. Another approach is to turn to an anthology of Greek literature to help you select a book or writer you would like to read. Good translations often have helpful introductions, but to learn more about your author's life and world, you can also use one of the many introductory books listed below.

In addition, some mythological handbooks survive from antiquity: Hesiod's *Theogony*, Apollodorus's *Library*, and the Roman poet Ovid's beautiful and masterful *Metamorphoses*, all available in English. Moral lessons illustrated by talking animals can, moreover, be found in the collected fables of Aesop.

It can also be an exciting and illuminating experience to visit an art museum that contains a collection of classical art. Ancient Greek vases were decorated like mythological comic books, and with the help of the Greek alphabet you may be able to decipher the names of some of your favorite heroes (though be advised that sometimes the vase-painters wrote from right to left!). Meanwhile the marble statues in the gallery will give you a three-dimensional impression of the gods and goddesses you've come to know.

While in the museum, be sure also to stroll down the galleries of later European art, especially from the Renaissance through the nineteenth century, eras that were visually influenced and deeply inspired by Greek myths and their creative power.

Greek Civilization

Amos, H.D., and Lang, A.G.P. *These Were the Greeks*. Chester Springs, PA: Dufour, 1979.

Brunschwig, Jacques, and Lloyd, Geoffrey E.R., eds. *Greek Thought: A Guide to Classical Knowledge*. Cambridge, MA: Harvard University Press, 2000.

Carpenter, Rhys. *The Esthetic Basis of Greek Art.* Bloomington, IN: Indiana University Press, 1959.

Cartledge, Paul. *The Cambridge Illustrated History of Ancient Greece.* New York: Cambridge University Press, 1998.

Dodds, E.R. *The Greeks and the Irrational.* Berkeley: University of California Press, 1951.

Durant, Will. *The Life of Greece.* New York: Simon & Schuster, 1966.

Freeman, Charles. *The Greek Achievement: The Foundation of the Western World.* New York: Viking Penguin, 1999.

Frost, Frank J., *Greek Society.* 5th ed. Boston: Houghton Mifflin, 1997.

Grant, Michael, ed. *Greek Literature: An Anthology.* New York: Penguin, 1990.

Hadas, Moses. *Ancilla to Classical Reading.* New York: Columbia University Press, 1954.

_____. *A History of Greek Literature.* New York: Columbia University Press, 1950.

_____. *Humanism: The Greek Ideal and Its Survival.* New York: Harper, 1960.

_____. *Old Wine, New Bottles: A Humanist Teacher at Work.* New York: Pocket Books, 1963.

Highet, Gilbert. *The Classical Tradition: Greek and Roman Influences on Western Literature.* New York: Oxford University Press, 1976.

Howatson, M.C., and Chilvers, Ian. *The Concise Oxford Companion to Classical Literature.* New York: Oxford University Press, 1993.

Jaeger, Werner. *Paideia: The Ideals of Greek Culture.* 3 vols. New York: Oxford University Press, 1965.

Kebric, Robert B. *Greek People.* 3rd ed. Mountain View, CA: Mayfield, 2001.

Kitto, H.D.F. *The Greeks.* New York: Penguin, 1957.

Knox, Bernard, ed. *The Norton Book of Classical Literature.* New York: Norton, 1993.

Nichols, Roger, and McLeish, Kenneth. *Through Greek Eyes: Greek Civilization in the Words of Greek Writers.* New York: Cambridge University Press, 1974.

Pomeroy, Sarah; Burnstein, Stanley M.; Donlan, Walter; and Roberts, Jennifer Tolbert. *Ancient Greece: A Political, Social, and Cultural History.* New York: Oxford University Press, 1999.

Spivey, Nigel. *Greek Art.* London: Phaidon, 1997.

Starr, Chester G. *The Ancient Greeks.* New York: Oxford University Press, 1971.

Woodford, Susan. *An Introduction to Greek Art.* Ithaca, NY: Cornell University Press, 1986.

Greek Mythology

Calasso, Roberto. *The Marriage of Cadmus and Harmony.* New York: Knopf, 1993.

DeNicola, Deborah, ed. *Orpheus and Company: Contemporary Poems on Greek Mythology.* Hanover, NH: University Press of New England, 1999.

Grant, Michael. *Myths of the Greeks and Romans.* Cleveland: World, 1962.

Hamilton, Edith. *Mythology.* New York: New American Library, 1942.

Harris, Stephen L. and Platzner, Gloria. *Classical Mythology: Insights and Images.* Mountain View, CA: Mayfield, 1998.

Henle, Jane. *Greek Myths: A Vase Painter's Notebook.* Bloomington, IN, 1973.

Kerényi, C. *The Gods of the Greeks.* New York: Grove, 1960.

_____. *The Heroes of the Greeks.* New York: Grove 1959.

Morford, Mark P.O., and Lenardon, Robert J. *Classical Mythology.* 6th ed. New York: Longman, 1999.

Peradotto, John. *Classical Mythology: An Annotated Bibliographical Survey.* Urbana, IL: American Philological Association, 1973.

Powell, Barry B. *Classical Myth.* 2nd ed. Englewood Cliffs, NJ: Prentice Hall, 1995.

Schwab, Gustav. *Gods & Heroes: Myths and Epics of Ancient Greece.* New York: Pantheon, 1974.

Veyne, Paul. *Did the Greeks Believe in Their Myths? An Essay on the Constitutive Imagination.* Chicago: University of Chicago Press, 1988.

Rome

Barrow, R.H. *The Romans.* New York: Penguin, 1949.

Bertman, Stephen. *Art and the Romans.* Lawrence, KS: Coronado, 1975.

Israel

Harris, Stephen L. *The New Testament: A Student's Introduction.* 3rd ed. Mountain View, CA: Mayfield, 1998.

Silver, Abba Hillel. *Where Judaism Differed.* New York: Macmillan, 1957.

Egypt

David, Rosalie. *Handbook to Life in Ancient Egypt.* New York: Facts On File, 1998.

Mertz, Barbara. *Red Land, Black Land: Daily Life in Ancient Egypt.* New York: Peter Bedrick, 1978.

Mesopotamia

Bertman, Stephen. *Handbook to Life in Ancient Mesopotamia.* New York: Facts On File, 2003.

Mason, Herbert, trans. *Gilgamesh: A Verse Narrative*. New York: New American Library, 1972.

About the Author

Stephen Bertman received his doctorate in Greek and Latin Literature from Columbia University, and holds additional degrees in Classics from New York University and in Near Eastern and Judaic Studies from Brandeis. Dr. Bertman has published extensively in the field of ancient Mediterranean civilization. In addition to articles and chapters on Classical and Near Eastern history and thought, his books include *Art and the Romans, Doorways through Time: The Romance of Archaeology*, and the *Handbook to Life in Ancient Mesopotamia*. He has also explored the challenges of contemporary civilization in *Hyperculture: The Human Cost of Speed* and *Cultural Amnesia: America's Future and the Crisis of Memory*.

As a teacher, writer, educational consultant, and public speaker, Dr. Bertman has dedicated his life to bridging the worlds of past and present. Stephen Bertman lives with his wife, Elaine, in West Bloomfield, Michigan.